100 Ways with Vegetables

Anne Ager

Letts**Guides**

Charles Letts and Company Ltd
London Edinburgh München and New York

First published 1976
2nd impression 1976
by Charles Letts and Company Limited
Diary House, Borough Road, London SE1 1DW

Design and illustrations by Ed Perera
Cover photograph by Andrew Thompson

Printed in Great Britain

Contents

Introduction

Vegetables are among the most varied and interesting of foods, and the most exciting as far as flavour, colour and texture are concerned. Often the most easily available vegetables are the most delicious: think of the rich earthy flavour of potatoes, the sweet fruitiness of tomatoes, the tang and bite of crisp onions. Yet the variety of vegetables available is enormous, and a large proportion come from other countries.

We are fortunate today to be able to buy a wide selection of foreign and rare vegetables. Prior to the sixteenth century the choice of vegetables was very limited in Europe—cabbage in its various forms, carrots and beetroot were the three most widely available. It was only with the growth of foreign trading, after Columbus's discovery of America in 1492, that a whole new vegetable world was thrown open to Europe: the potato was an unsampled delicacy, until Sir Walter Raleigh returned from his voyage to the New World in the sixteenth century. It is now an everyday staple food. Many other new vegetables made their appearance about the same time: for example brussels sprouts, runner beans, spinach and celery.

The vegetable family is split into four main sections:
bulbs, e.g. onions, fennel;
green leaf, e.g. cabbage, lettuce, spinach;
roots and tubers, e.g. carrots, swedes, potatoes;
seeds and pulses, e.g. peas, beans;
fungi, including mushrooms, are a group on their own. In this country we generally eat only mushrooms from this group.

There are also numerous vegetables, for example asparagus and tomatoes, which are unique and do not fall into any specific category.

The seasons of vegetables vary considerably, depending on their planting season, the amount of sunlight they require and the length of time that they need to grow. I have purposely chosen recipes for six vegetables that are available all the year round: cabbage, carrots, mushrooms, onions, potatoes and tomatoes. All are grown in this country and we import other varieties from abroad to supplement supplies. We can buy Dutch tomatoes, for example, when the production in our own country is low or affected by bad weather.

The storage of vegetables is particularly important for maintaining their peak freshness. The secret is to buy the freshest vegetables available. The atmosphere in which they are stored should be cool and well ventilated. Ideally they should be kept in a vegetable rack so that the air has a chance to circulate between them. Highly perishable vegetables, such as mushrooms and lettuce, are best stored in the 'crisper' draw of the refrigerator. Root vegetables, such as carrots and potatoes, have a much longer shelf life; they can be bought up to a week in advance.

Vegetables play a very important part in our daily diet. Apart from being an excellent source of readily available vitamins (for example A, B, C and D), they also provide necessary roughage because of their cellular structure.

To get the maximum nutritional value from vegetables eat them raw: there are few vegetables that can't be served in their raw state. Mixed vegetable salads are colourful and their crunch and bite contrast pleasantly in texture with more bland, smooth foods. Serve raw chopped or grated vegetables in a simple dressing that doesn't mask their characteristic flavours, and prepare them only a short while before eating. Root vegetables are best grated or finely sliced, whereas leaf vegetables only require fine shredding One of the simplest and most effective ways of presenting vegetables is in the form of crudités (French style). This is a selection of raw chopped vegetables served with mayonnaise or a vinaigrette dressing (see pp 15, 32). Crudités can be served on many occasions, as an accompaniment to drinks, as a table centre-piece or as a starter to a meal. They are also an ideal between-meal snack for slimmers.

The method of cooking vegetables is just as important as maintaining their freshness. It is easy to overcook vegetables, thus ruining their texture, colour and flavour. The English are renowned for reducing them to an inedible 'mush' by soaking them in advance and then cooking them in excess water for a prolonged time. Most of the goodness of root and tuber vegetables lies just beneath the skin: peel them only when absolutely necessary, that is, when they are particularly old. Most surface dirt can be removed quite easily by scrubbing or rinsing them quickly, rather than soaking them in a sinkful of water.

To appreciate their full flavour, there is no better way of serving vegetables than simply cooked, either boiled or baked, with melted butter or a complementary sauce. The shorter the boiling time the better. Cut vegetables which are on the tough side into smaller pieces before cooking. Cook them in a covered pan, in as little liquid as possible. This means that their flavour is not lost in evaporation, and they retain a good shape. Wherever possible use the cooking liquid in gravy or a sauce so that none of the goodness is wasted. Try the following suggestions as variations to the normal boiling method. Instead of water use stock or add a squeeze of lemon juice or white wine to the cooking liquid, or add some herbs, a bay leaf or finely chopped onion to the pot.

Baking vegetables both saves fuel and cooks them gently. Prepare the vegetables and put them into a shallow oven-proof dish. Add very little water or stock, seasoning and a knob of butter. Cover with a lid or foil, and cook gently in a moderate oven, underneath a casserole or roast.

Vegetable dishes can also make substantial and satisfying main meals at a very economical price, for example, baked onions with a savoury stuffing, casseroled tomatoes or potatoes layered with onions and cheese.

There are further suggestions for substantial dishes in the main recipe sections of the book. Each of these sections deals with one vegetable: cabbage, carrots, mushrooms, onions, potatoes and tomatoes, and the recipes given are for soups or starters, simple vegetable dishes and main dishes, in that order.

Vegetable guide

What do they look like, when are they in season, and how do you use them? This is a guide to many common and rare vegetables, including the six featured in this book.

The seasons given are a general guide. As many vegetables are now imported and force-grown, they tend to be more readily available.

Artichoke, globe (June–September) A small inedible fibrous core or 'choke', surrounded by small pointed green leaves; the leaves are pulled off the cooked artichoke and dipped into hot melted butter, or served cold with vinaigrette. The 'heart' can be removed and used in salads.

Artichokes, Jerusalem (March–July) These are quite different to the globe variety; they are tubers from a type of sunflower and resemble a small knobbly parsnip in shape. They are best parboiled and then baked, as they tend to cook unevenly.

Asparagus (April–July) A green stem vegetable usually imported, as the British climate is not suitable for growing asparagus. It is normally cooked tied together in bundles, preferably in a steamer.

Aubergine (nearly all the year round) A shiny purplish-black vegetable, either long and pear-shaped, or oval:

aubergine is usually sliced and sprinkled with salt before frying, to remove excess water and the slightly bitter flavour. Halved aubergines, for baking, are scored and sprinkled with salt.

Beans, broad (April–July)
The beans are tightly packed in large green pods with a furry lining. The beans are removed from the pods before cooking.

Beans, French (mainly April–June)
These beans are smaller and more delicate and tender than runner beans. They only need topping and tailing before cooking.

Beans, runner (March–June)
These are long, wide green beans which are cut into thin diagonal slices before being cooked.

Cabbage, spring (February–June)
Tender green cabbage with a smooth shiny leaf; it needs gentle, light cooking (see also p 14).

Cabbage, winter (October–April)
Firm-textured green cabbage, with a slightly curly leaf, sometimes purplish at the ends; it is tougher than spring cabbage, and takes longer to cook (see also p 14).

Cabbage, red (nearly all the year round)
Dark, deep red-leafed cabbage, with closely packed leaves; used mainly in this country for pickling. On the Continent it is cooked with apple and spices as a hot vegetable (see also p 14).

Cabbage, white (all the year round)
Firmly packed crisp white cabbage, which stores very well; shredded white cabbage can be cooked as a hot vegetable, or mixed with mayonnaise for coleslaw (see also p 14).

Capsicums (nearly all the year round)
More commonly known as red and green peppers, or pimentos; both are shiny smooth-skinned ridged vegetables. The green variety has a slightly bitter flavour, while the red capsicum is sweet. They are used raw in salads and in many hot dishes.

Carrots (nearly all the year round; young carrots in spring)
Long tapered, orange root vegetable, with a crisp sweet flavour; used as a basic ingredient in many dishes: soups, sauces, casseroles and so on (see also pp 22–23).

Cauliflower (nearly all the year round; at their best from November to June).
A large head of tightly packed white florets; can either be cooked whole, or separated into florets. Broccoli is a member of the same family, but the most common variety here is deep purplish-green in colour, less compact, and grows on long stems.

Celeriac (September–March)
This is a type of celery root. It can be cooked like swede or used in soups,

and is also very good grated raw in salads.

Celery (nearly all the year round)
A long-stemmed crisp light green vegetable, with fresh crinkly leaves; it has a refreshing watery flavour, and the crispness is best appreciated if eaten raw. It is, however, used in many cooked dishes, particularly soups.

Chicory (September–May)
Crisp white leaves, with yellow tips, tightly packed in 'bullet' shapes; it is sometimes braised, but is best eaten raw. It discolours very quickly.

Corn on the cob (July–October)
A long fibrous core (cob), studded with small tightly packed yellow corn kernels; it can either be cooked whole, as a starter or vegetable, or the kernels can be removed from the cob before cooking.

Courgette (June–September)
The baby member of the marrow family, usually about 4 in long; salting before frying or baking (see aubergine) helps to take away the slightly bitter flavour of the skin. Very tough skin can be removed before cooking.

Cucumber (all the year round)
Long shiny green vegetable, with a sweetish watery flavour; its green peel is slightly bitter. It is usually sliced or chopped in salads, but can also be cooked.

Endive (almost all the year round)
A crinkly, frilly 'lettuce', variegated green in colour, with a slightly bitter flavour; used in the same way as lettuce, for salads.

Leeks (September–April)
Leeks are long, slender, green and white vegetables, with bulbous roots; they have a strong characteristic flavour, somewhat similar to onion. They add a good flavour to soups and stews.

Lettuce (all the year round, depending on type: Cos, Cabbage and Romaine)
All have green leaves, but the Cos variety has very long smooth darkish-green leaves, tougher in texture than the more crinkly Romaine and Cabbage types. Lettuce is usually eaten as salad, but can be cooked.

Marrow (June–October)
A large dark green bulbous vegetable with paler ridged stripes; the inside flesh is delicate, pale in colour, and very watery. The centre is a mass of edible pips. Either hollowed and stuffed or cooked in slices.

Mushrooms (all the year round)
They are a variety of edible fungi. The three main varieties are flat, cup and button. The button variety is often used raw in salads. The characteristic flavour of mushrooms is added to many dishes: fish, meat,

poultry and so on (see also pp 30–31).

Onions (all the year round, apart from shallots)
All types have basically the same structure: a fleshy white bulb, slightly pointed at one end. The onions with a pinkish tinge tend to be stronger than those with a brownish skin. Onions are used in many different ways and must easily be the most widely used vegetable (see also pp 38–39).

Parsnips (September–April)
Cultivated parsnips, not wild ones, are eaten. They are root vegetables, creamy yellow in colour and rather like a fat carrot in shape; used in similar dishes to carrots, swedes and turnips.

Peas (June–October)
Peas are enclosed in pale green pods —the young, thin peas can be cooked as they are, in their shucks, but the older, more bulbous pods must be removed and the shelled peas cooked separately.

Potatoes (all year round, apart from the new young potatoes)
Firm, starchy root vegetables, with a rough brownish skin, and white waxy centre; the peel is removed from old potatoes before cooking, but is usually left on the new ones (see also pp 45–47).

Pumpkin (September–November)
This is a member of the gourd family. A ridged, circular vegetable, with a tough brownish-orange skin, and a paler orange fleshy centre, containing seeds. The Americans use its bland flavour in sweet dishes, but it can also be cooked as a savoury vegetable.

Radishes (April–October)
Small bright reddish-purple root vegetables, with crisp white flesh and a slightly hot peppery flavour; used mainly in salads or as a garnish.

Spinach (April–November)
A green leaf vegetable, which is one of the richest sources of iron. It needs very thorough washing, and the stalk should be removed; used raw in salads or cooked in very little water.

Sprouts (August–April)
Brussels sprouts resemble miniature compact cabbages, and grow in clusters on a thick stalk. A cross is cut in the base of each one before cooking, to ensure that they are cooked evenly (see also p 14).

Swedes (September–May)
A member of the turnip family, the swede is a large, firm root vegetable with a brownish skin, and yellow-orange flesh. It needs to be peeled thickly and kept under water, to prevent discoloration. Cut into pieces before cooking.

Sweet potato (September–April)
This is the tuber from a creeping vine; it has a reddish purple skin, with a sweet yellow flesh. It can be

cooked like an ordinary potato or used in other savoury dishes.

Tomato (all year round)
The tomato is a soft fleshy fruit, with a slightly sweet flavour. Its bright red colour is added to many cooked and raw dishes (see also pp 54–56).

Turnips (all year round)
Turnips have a coarse, greenish-white outer skin with a milky-white watery flesh, rather cellular in texture. The small ones can be cooked whole in stews or casseroles; the larger ones should be cut into pieces.

Freezing vegetables and made-up vegetable dishes

Ideally vegetables should be frozen within a few hours of being picked, but this is neither possible nor practical for most of us. We can, however, be careful how we choose and buy our vegetables for freezing. It is worth selecting good quality vegetables that are in tiptop condition and free from blemishes—damaged vegetables will freeze unsuccessfully. There is one exception to this rule: tomatoes. Bruised or very soft tomatoes can be cooked to a pulp and frozen, to be used as a base for sauces, soups and casseroles.

The general principle for freezing vegetables is to first wash them, peeling or scraping if necessary.

Sort into similar sizes, or cut into desired shapes, for example, cut potatoes as chips. Blanch in boiling water, to prevent the chemical changes which cause vegetables to lose colour and deteriorate in quality. After blanching, cool the vegetables quickly in iced water, and then drain them well.

Freezing the six selected vegetables in this book

Cabbage: use only young cabbage. Trim off outer coarse leaves. Wash in salted water and cut or tear into shreds. Blanch in boiling water for $1\frac{1}{2}$ minutes. Cool quickly in iced water and drain. Pack into waxed cartons or freezer bags and seal to exclude the air. Label and freeze. Can be stored for up to 6 months.

Carrots: wash carrots. Scrape or peel, and either leave whole, or cut into dice. Blanch in boiling water for 4 minutes. Cool quickly in iced water and drain. Pack into waxed cartons or freezer bags, and seal to exclude the air. Label and freeze. Can be stored for up to 8 months.

Mushrooms: if mushrooms are larger than 1 in in diameter, they should be sliced or quartered. Wash mushrooms and drain. Dry on a clean tea towel. Sauté in butter for 1 minute. Drain well and cool. Pack into waxed cartons and seal to exclude the air. Label and freeze. Can be stored for up to 10 months.

Onions: peel onions, and slice or chop finely. Small onions can be frozen whole. Blanch in boiling water: 2 minutes for chopped onion, 4 minutes for whole. Cool quickly in iced water and drain. Pack into waxed cartons and seal to exclude the air. Overwrap in freezer wrap to prevent the strong smell penetrating other foods. Label and freeze. Can be stored for up to 3 months.

Potatoes: wash and peel potatoes. Keep whole, slice, or cut into chips. Blanch in boiling water for 2 minutes. Cool quickly in iced water and drain. Pack into freezer bags and seal to exclude the air. Label and freeze. Can be stored for up to 12 months.

Tomatoes: whole tomatoes tend to become soft after freezing, and are best frozen sliced, chopped, as a puree, or as a juice. Blanching is unnecessary. Pack into waxed cartons and seal to exclude the air. Label and freeze. Can be stored for up to 10 months.

All these vegetables can be cooked from their frozen state. Cook for less time than fresh vegetables, as the blanching process reduces the time needed to cook through.

Correct packaging of frozen food is essential and cannot be over-emphasized—faulty packaging will cause loss of quality through drying out and flavour transference from one food to another. Materials must be moisture and vapour-proof, and packages must be sealed tightly. Labelling is also important, to guarantee that the vegetables are used within their storage time.

For freezing made-up vegetable dishes, choose a container that suits the type of dish: waxed cartons for very liquid foods, such as soups and sauces; foil pie dishes for pies (cook and freeze in the same container); large lidded foil dishes for casseroles, baked dishes and so on (they can then be reheated in the same container); individual freezer cartons for small portion foods such as pates.

Weights and measures

All ingredient quantities are given in British Standard measurements, and the appropriate American measures for each ingredient follow at the foot of every recipe. Note that American spoon measures are smaller than British spoons:

1 British teaspoon equals $1\frac{1}{4}$ American teaspoons
1 British tablespoon equals $1\frac{1}{4}$ American tablespoons.

The following metric equivalents apply for measuring ingredients, but note that metric measures are always given as convenient round figures and are only approximate equivalents. When converting large quantities one obtains slightly less of the finished product than when using ounces and pounds.

1 oz is taken as 25gm
4 oz are taken as 100gm
8 oz are taken as 200gm

1 lb is taken as 400gm
1 teaspoon is taken as 5ml (American teasp 4·8ml)
1 tablespoon is taken as 15m¹ (American tbsp 14·8ml)
$\frac{1}{4}$ pint is taken as 150ml
1 pint is taken as 600ml
2 pints are taken as 1 litre

Equivalent oven temperatures

250°F	Mark $\frac{1}{2}$	130°C
275°F	Mark 1	140°C
300°F	Mark 2	145°C
325°F	Mark 3	160°C
350°F	Mark 4	175°C
375°F	Mark 5	190°C
400°F	Mark 6	205°C
425°F	Mark 7	220°C
450°F	Mark 8	235°C

Abbreviations
teasp—teaspoon
tbsp—tablespoon

All recipes that are marked with a star * are particularly suitable for freezing.

Cabbage

The horticultural term for cultivated cabbages is brassicas, but the word cabbage is a shortened version of cabbage-cole, a corruption of the Latin *caput* (head) and *cole* (stalk), thus meaning stalk with a big head. The cabbage has been a popular European vegetable for more than three centuries. The Arabs grew cabbages in the thirteenth and fourteenth centuries, and they eventually came to England in the seventeenth century via Cyprus, in seed form. There are many different varieties of cabbage but only a few are eaten regularly in this country.

Brussels sprouts, a member of the cabbage family, were not introduced into this country until the early nineteenth century. They originated in Belgium; hence their name. The most popular varieties of brassicas are as follows

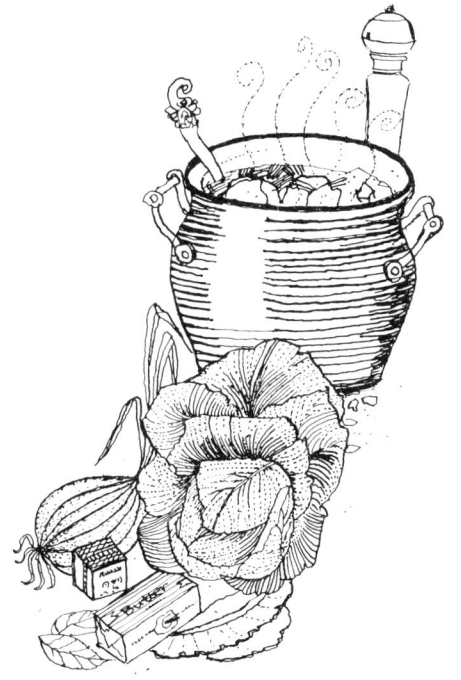

round cabbage: the firm, round, green cabbage, often called winter cabbage; **spring cabbage:** the loose-leafed cabbage which is closely allied to spring greens. These have practically no heart at all and are much smaller plants than the fully grown cabbages.

Red cabbage: tightly-packed, firm, deep purple cabbage; this is often used in coleslaw (raw cabbage salad) and as the base for sauerkraut.

Broccoli: tight, purplish-green, white or green flowers surrounded by green leaves; **cauliflower** has white flowers surrounded by green leaves and is very closely allied to broccoli.

Kale: crinkly-leafed green cabbage, resembling giant parsley; **brussels sprouts** are like tiny, compact cabbages, about the size of a walnut.

Most members of the cabbage family are available throughout the year, with the exception of red cabbage. This is at its most plentiful in the winter months.

All fresh brassicas will keep for a week, if stored in a cool dry place. Firm white and red cabbages will keep up to a fortnight.

Cabbage has a higher vitamin C content than any other vegetable, and is a valuable part of our diet.

It should be very carefully prepared and cooked: rinse but do not soak it. Soaking destroys the goodness, as vitamin C is water-soluble. For simple cooking, discard any hard outer leaves and the hard core of the stalk and put the leaves, whole or shredded, in a pan. Add as little water as possible, to prevent sticking, and cover the pan. Cook fast for about ten minutes. Wherever possible, use the cabbage liquid as a base for a soup or gravy. This method should also be used for brussels sprouts and broccoli.

Baked cabbage is delicious. Pack shredded cabbage into a buttered casserole with a little chopped onion and seasoning. Add a scant $\frac{1}{4}$ pint (American: $\frac{1}{2}$ cup) stock with a tbsp of vinegar to bring out the flavour, and a good knob of butter. Cover the casserole and cook in a moderate oven for about $\frac{3}{4}$ hour, until the cabbage is just tender.

Most of the following green cabbage recipes can be used for brussels sprouts or broccoli. In place of one small cabbage, use $\frac{3}{4}$ lb–1 lb of sprouts or broccoli (American: $2\frac{1}{2}$–3 cups).

*Cabbage soup

Serves 4–6
2 onions sliced
1 clove crushed garlic
2 oz butter
1 tbsp oil
$\frac{1}{2}$ small green cabbage
2 potatoes
seasoning
$1\frac{1}{4}$ pints stock
2 rashers crispy fried bacon

Fry the sliced onion and garlic gently in the butter and oil for 5 minutes. Add the finely shredded cabbage and continue frying over a gentle heat, stirring continuously. Add the peeled and thinly sliced potatoes, seasoning and stock. Bring to the boil, and simmer covered for $\frac{1}{2}$ hour. Adjust seasoning. Serve piping hot, topped with the chopped bacon, and accompanied by crusty bread.

This is an ideal opportunity to use up stale French bread: spread the sliced bread with butter, and pop into a moderate oven for 15 minutes.

(American: $\frac{1}{4}$ cup butter, generous $2\frac{1}{2}$ cups stock)

Cabbage tartare

Serves 6
1 small green cabbage
seasoning
4 tbsp mayonnaise (see below)
1 tbsp capers
2 pickled cucumbers, chopped

Remove any tough stalk from the cabbage. Chop the cabbage very coarsely. Put into a pan with $\frac{1}{4}$ pint boiling water and seasoning. Cover pan and bring back to the boil. Simmer until cabbage is just tender. Drain thoroughly. Return cabbage to the pan with mayonnaise, capers and pickled cucumber. Heat through gently.

(American: $\frac{1}{2}$ cup water)

For the mayonnaise:

Makes $\frac{1}{2}$ pint
2 egg yolks
$\frac{1}{2}$ pint oil
1 tbsp vinegar or lemon juice
1 teasp made mustard
seasoning
pinch caster sugar
little hot water

Beat egg yolks thoroughly in a bowl with the vinegar—this prevents the mustard 'burning' the egg. Mix in the mustard. Add the oil very gradually, in a slow trickle, beating vigorously all the time. Once all the oil has been incorporated, add seasoning and sugar to taste, and if necessary, thin mayonnaise with a little hot water.

(American: 1 cup oil)

Hot cabbage slaw

Serves 6
1 small white cabbage
1 peeled onion, stuck with a clove
small piece streaky bacon
bay leaf
seasoning
2 oz butter
1 tbsp oil
1 onion
1 apple
2 oz raisins

Remove the thick stubby piece of stalk from the white cabbage. Shred the cabbage finely. Put the cabbage into a pan with the onion and clove, bay leaf and seasoning. Add $\frac{1}{2}$ pint water and bring to the boil. Cover pan and simmer for 15 minutes. The cabbage should still be slightly crisp. Drain thoroughly. Heat butter and oil and add the finely sliced onion. Fry gently for 5 minutes. Add the cooked cabbage, the cored and sliced apple, and raisins. Toss over a low heat for 5 minutes, until heated through.

(American: 4 tbsp butter, $\frac{1}{2}$ cup raisins, generous cup of water)

Cabbage en persillade

Serves 6
1 small green cabbage
$\frac{1}{4}$ pint stock
seasoning
2 oz butter
1 clove crushed garlic
1 teasp sugar
3 tbsp chopped parsley

Remove any tough stalk from the cabbage. Shred cabbage finely. Put into a pan with the hot stock and seasoning. Cover pan and bring to the boil. Simmer gently until the cabbage is just tender. Drain thoroughly. Put cabbage into a hot serving dish and keep warm. Melt butter and fry garlic gently for 1 minute. Stir in the sugar, parsley and cabbage cooking liquid. Bring to the boil. Pour over the cabbage and serve immediately.

(American: generous $\frac{1}{2}$ cup stock, 4 tbsp butter)

Cabbage with fresh cream

Serves 6
1 small green cabbage
$\frac{1}{4}$ pint stock
$1\frac{1}{2}$ oz butter
seasoning
$\frac{1}{4}$ pint double cream
ground nutmeg

Cut cabbage into 6 even sections, removing any tough stalk. Put the cabbage sections into a shallow pan with the hot stock, butter and seasoning. Cover pan and bring to the boil. Simmer until the cabbage is just tender—most of the liquid will evaporate during cooking. Stir in the cream and a generous pinch of nutmeg. Heat through. This tastes particularly good if sprinkled with a little coarsely grated cheese just before serving.

(American: generous $\frac{1}{2}$ cup stock, generous $\frac{1}{2}$ cup cream, 3 tbsp butter)

Sweet sour cabbage

Serves 6
1 small green cabbage
1 small can pineapple chunks
1 tbsp honey
2 tbsp vinegar
1 onion
1 oz chopped nuts

Remove any tough stalk from the cabbage. Shred cabbage coarsely. Drain the pineapple chunks, and measure off $\frac{1}{4}$ pint of the juice. Put the shredded cabbage into a pan. Heat the pineapple juice with the honey, vinegar, chopped onion and seasoning. Pour over the cabbage. Cover the pan and bring to the boil. Simmer until the cabbage is just tender. Drain cabbage and toss with chopped pineapple chunks and nuts.

(American: 1 cup pineapple chunks, 2 tbsp chopped nuts, generous $\frac{1}{2}$ cup pineapple juice)

Cabbage with burnt sugar

Serves 6
1 small green cabbage
seasoning
2 oz butter
2 oz demerara sugar

Remove any tough stalk from the cabbage. Shred cabbage very finely. Put into a pan with $\frac{1}{4}$ pint hot water and the seasoning. Cover the pan and bring to the boil. Simmer until cabbage is just tender. Drain thoroughly. Toss cabbage in the butter. Put into a greased ovenproof dish. Sprinkle with the demerara sugar. Put under a hot grill for 3–4 minutes, until the sugar caramelizes. Take care that it does not actually burn.

(American: $\frac{1}{4}$ cup butter, 4 tbsp demerara sugar, generous $\frac{1}{2}$ cup water)

Cabbage with orange

Serves 4–6
1 small red cabbage
$\frac{1}{2}$ pint stock
1 orange
seasoning
1 tbsp orange marmalade
1 oz butter

Remove any hard core from the cabbage—the stalk is very thick on a red cabbage. Shred the cabbage very finely, using a sharp knife. Put shredded cabbage into a pan. Heat the stock with the grated orange rind and seasoning. Pour over the cabbage. Cover the pan and bring to the boil. Simmer until just tender. Meanwhile, remove all the pith and membrane from the orange and chop the flesh. Drain the cabbage thoroughly. Return cooked cabbage to a clean pan and add the orange marmalade, the chopped orange and the butter. Heat through.

(American: generous cup stock, 2 tbsp butter)

*Cabbage au gratin

Serves 6
1 small green cabbage
seasoning
$1\frac{1}{2}$ oz butter
$\frac{1}{2}$ pint white sauce
2 tbsp cream
3 oz grated cheese

Remove any tough stalk from the cabbage. Shred the cabbage coarsely. Put cabbage into a pan with $\frac{1}{4}$ pint hot water and the seasoning. Cover the pan and bring to the boil. Simmer until the cabbage is just tender. Drain thoroughly. Toss the cabbage in butter. Put into a well greased ovenproof dish. Heat the white sauce and add the cream and 2 oz of the cheese. Spoon evenly over the cabbage. Sprinkle with the remaining cheese. Put under a hot grill for a few minutes, until the cheese bubbles and browns. This can be done in a moderate oven, in which

case it will take about 15 minutes.

(American: 3 tbsp butter, generous cup white sauce, $\frac{3}{4}$ cup grated cheese, generous $\frac{1}{2}$ cup water)

*Cabbage pancakes

Serves 4
It is essential that the cabbage in these pancakes is crisp and slightly crunchy—it should not be actually cooked right through.

$\frac{1}{2}$ small green cabbage
2 oz butter
2 tbsp oil
1 grated onion
$\frac{1}{4}$ pint milk
$\frac{1}{4}$ pint water
4 oz flour
pinch salt
1 egg
cayenne pepper
cream cheese

Remove any tough stalk from the cabbage. Shred cabbage finely. Fry in the butter and oil for about 5–6 minutes. Mix with the onion and allow to cool. Mix a little of the milk and water with the sieved flour and salt and the egg. Beat until smooth, and then gradually beat in the remaining liquid. Stir cabbage mixture into the batter. Heat a large pancake or frying pan and add enough oil or fat to give a thin even coating. Spoon in a ladleful of the cabbage batter—sufficient to give a generous coating of the base of the pan. Cook until set and golden on the underside. Flip the pancake over and cook on the other side. Repeat with the remaining batter, making 8 pancakes in all. Serve hot with cream cheese.

(American: $\frac{1}{4}$ cup butter, $\frac{1}{2}$ cup milk, $\frac{1}{2}$ cup water, 1 cup flour)

First day bubble and squeak

Serves 6
Bubble and squeak is usually made from left-over cooked vegetables. In this recipe they are cooked freshly, on the same day.

1 small green cabbage
3 medium potatoes
seasoning
1 onion, sliced
2 oz butter
2 tbsp oil

Remove any tough pieces of stalk from the cabbage. Shred cabbage coarsely. Peel potatoes and cut into thick slices, approx. $\frac{1}{4}$ in thick. Put shredded cabbage and sliced potato into a pan. Add $\frac{1}{2}$ pint water and seasoning. Cover pan and simmer gently until vegetables are just tender. Drain thoroughly. Fry the sliced onion in butter and oil for 5 minutes. Add the drained cabbage and potato, and fry gently until lightly golden and crisp.

(American: $\frac{1}{4}$ cup butter, generous cup of water)

*Cabbage and onion pie

Serves 6
1 small green cabbage
2 onions, sliced
seasoning
$\frac{1}{4}$ pint stock
$\frac{3}{4}$ lb potatoes
2 oz butter
2 tbsp cream
2 oz grated cheese

Remove any tough stalk from the cabbage. Shred cabbage coarsely. Put into a pan with the sliced onion, seasoning and stock. Cover pan and bring to the boil. Simmer until the cabbage is just tender. Meanwhile, peel and roughly chop the potatoes. Cook in boiling salted water until just tender. Drain potatoes well and mash with the butter, cream and seasoning, until smooth and creamy. Mix in the grated cheese. Put the cooked cabbage into a greased ovenproof dish. Spoon potato evenly over the cabbage. Bake at Mark 5, 375°F, for 25 minutes. To make this a more substantial main meal dish, add 6 oz chopped cooked meat to the cabbage, before topping with potato.

(American: generous $\frac{1}{2}$ cup stock, 2 cups cooked potato, $\frac{1}{4}$ cup butter, 4 tbsp grated cheese, 1 generous cup cooked chopped meat)

Braised cabbage with bacon

Serves 6
1 small green cabbage
2 oz butter
1 onion
3 rashers bacon
bay leaf
seasoning
$\frac{1}{2}$ pint stock

Remove any tough stalk from the cabbage. Cut cabbage into 6 equal sections. Put half the chopped onion into the base of a greased casserole. Lay the cabbage sections on top. Add the butter, cut into small pieces, the chopped bacon, bay leaf, stock, seasoning and the remaining onion. Cover casserole with a lid or a piece of foil. Cook at Mark 4, 350°F, for 45–50 minutes, until cabbage is just tender. Brown ale can be used instead of stock if liked.

(American: 4 tbsp butter, generous cup of stock)

Cabbage and sausage hotpot

This recipe is based on a favourite German dish in which a very coarse textured sausage is used instead of black pudding.

Serves 4–6
1 small green cabbage
$\frac{1}{2}$ lb black pudding
seasoning
1 onion
$\frac{1}{3}$ pint brown ale
few juniper berries

Remove any tough stalk from the cabbage. Shred cabbage coarsely. Cut black pudding into $\frac{1}{4}$ in thick slices, and slice the onion. Layer cabbage in a greased casserole with the black pudding, onion, seasoning and juniper berries. Pour the brown ale over the top. Cover the casserole with a lid or a piece of foil. Cook at Mark 3, 325°F, 1$\frac{1}{2}$ hours. Check that the liquid does not evaporate during cooking, and the cabbage become dry—if necessary, add a little extra liquid.

(American: 1$\frac{1}{2}$ cups sliced black pudding, $\frac{2}{3}$ cup brown ale)

Cabbage provencale

Serves 6
1 small green cabbage
1 onion
$\frac{1}{4}$ pint red wine
seasoning
1 clove crushed garlic
2 rashers bacon
1 tbsp oil
4 tomatoes, chopped
1 tbsp tomato puree
2 oz black olives

Remove any tough stalk from the cabbage. Shred cabbage coarsely. Put cabbage into a pan with the chopped onion, wine and seasoning.

Cover the pan and bring to the boil. Simmer gently until the cabbage is just tender. Drain the cabbage thoroughly, and keep it warm. Fry the garlic and the chopped bacon in oil for 3 minutes. Add the chopped tomatoes, the tomato puree and the liquid from cooking the cabbage. Bring to the boil. Add the olives and pour over the cabbage.

(American: $\frac{1}{2}$ cup red wine, $\frac{1}{4}$ cup black olives)

*Stuffed cabbage leaves

These are very similar to dolmas*; the Greeks, however, use vine leaves instead of cabbage, and usually rice in the filling.*

Serves 4
1 small cabbage
2 oz butter
2 tbsp oil
1 onion
1 clove crushed garlic
4 oz cooked meat
seasoning
2 tbsp breadcrumbs
1 egg yolk
14 oz can tomatoes
1 chicken stock cube

Remove 8 well-shaped outer cabbage leaves. Cut away the thick stubby centre spine from each of the cabbage leaves. Finely shred the remaining cabbage, discarding the tough stalk. Melt the butter and oil in a pan, and add the shredded cabbage, chopped onion and crushed garlic. Saute gently for 5 minutes. Plunge the outer leaves into a pan of boiling water for a few minutes, to make them more pliable. Mix the sauteed cabbage with the chopped cooked meat, seasoning and breadcrumbs. Bind with the egg yolk. Divide into 4 even portions. Enclose each portion of filling in 2 cabbage leaves, wrapping the ends over. Secure with wooden cocktail sticks. Place the stuffed cabbage leaves in a greased ovenproof dish. Add the tomatoes and the crumbled stock cube. Cook at Mark 4, 350°F, for 45–50 minutes. Baste the stuffed cabbage leaves during cooking to prevent them becoming dry.

(American: 4 tbsp butter, 1 cup chopped cooked meat, $1\frac{1}{2}$ cups canned tomatoes)

Carrots

The carrot is one of our most popular vegetables. The crisp texture of raw carrots and their characteristic orange colour appeals to adults and children alike. Carrots came into prominence during the Middle Ages when vegetables, woodland plants and herbs were used both by the apothecary, for medicinal purposes, and by the cook. The Normans discovered that carrots could be stored successfully in dry sand or earth, and this contributed to their usefulness and popularity.

The different types of carrot we can buy today are:
the larger, stubby, **old carrot**;
the smaller, **new carrot**;
the slim, regular-shaped imported carrots, for example those from California.

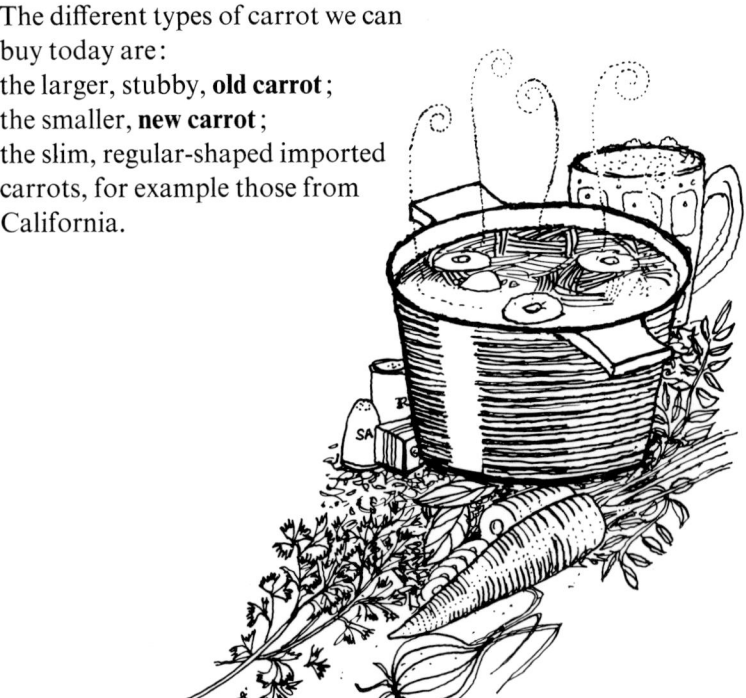

Older carrots are available all the year, while new carrots start their season at the beginning of the year and last through the spring. Imported carrots come into the country when our own young carrots are out of season.

Store carrots in a cool place, and keep them as dry as possible. Remove any excess dirt from them, which encourages damp and possible rotting, before storing.

Carrots contain vitamins A and C, and it is worth remembering this when preparing them. Peel old carrots to remove their rather tough outer skin, but only scrape or scrub young spring carrots. Never leave them soaking in cold water, as all their vitamin C will be lost. When cooking them use as little liquid as possible in order to retain the maximum food value.

Remember that carrots are as good raw as they are cooked—and it is far healthier for a child to nibble a raw carrot than to suck endless sweets. Use carrots in salads and sandwich fillings: grate them coarsely and toss in French dressing, orange or lemon juice, or mix with a little mayonnaise or cream cheese and sandwich between slices of bread.

The best method of cooking carrots is to put whole young carrots, or peeled and sliced old ones, into a pan with sufficient water to just cover the bottom. Add seasoning and a generous knob of butter. Cover the pan either with a lid or a piece of buttered paper, and cook over a low heat until the carrots are just tender. There will be very little excess liquid left, and this can be poured over the cooked carrots.

*Carrot and orange soup

Serves 6
1 lb carrots, peeled and grated
1 pint chicken stock
grated rind 2 oranges
seasoning
1 onion, finely chopped
1 teasp brown sugar
$\frac{1}{4}$ pint cream
thin slices of orange

Put grated carrot into a pan with the stock, grated orange rind, seasoning, chopped onion and brown sugar. Cover pan. Bring to the boil and simmer for $\frac{1}{2}$ hour. Either push the soup through a sieve, or, preferably, blend in a liquidizer until smooth. If you sieve the soup it will have a much coarser texture. Stir in the cream. Reheat the soup gently, to serve hot, or chill it for 2–3 hours, to serve cold. Float the orange slices on top of the soup.

(American: $1\frac{1}{2}$ cups grated carrot, 2 cups chicken stock, generous $\frac{1}{2}$ cup of cream)

Carrot shavings

This recipe is equally suitable for parsnips or potatoes.

Serves 4
5 large carrots
4 tbsp mayonnaise (see p 15)
seasoning
2 tbsp capers

Peel the carrots. Using a potato peeler, cut the peeled carrots into thin shavings: run the peeler down the carrots, lengthways, making long strips. Drop into a pan of boiling salted water and cook for 2 minutes. Drain thoroughly. Put mayonnaise into a small pan. Add the drained carrot shavings, seasoning and capers, and heat through.

Carrot slaw

Serves 4–6
4 large carrots, peeled and coarsely grated
2 eating apples, cored and finely chopped
4 lettuce leaves, finely shredded
1 oz chopped nuts
seasoning
mayonnaise (see p 00)

Mix the grated carrot with the finely chopped apple, shredded lettuce and chopped nuts. Add seasoning, and sufficient mayonnaise to bind. Serve with hot or cold meats. To serve with lamb, add a little redcurrant jelly; to serve with beef, a little creamed horseradish; and to serve with pork, a little apple chutney.

(American: 1 tbsp chopped nuts)

*Carrot mousse

Serves 4
4 oz cream cheese
grated rind $\frac{1}{2}$ orange
seasoning
pinch grated nutmeg
1 onion, grated
1 clove crushed garlic
2 large carrots, peeled and grated
$\frac{1}{4}$ pint double cream

Soften the cream cheese in a bowl with a wooden spoon. Add the grated orange rind, the seasoning and grated nutmeg. Beat in the grated onion, crushed garlic, and the grated carrot. Fold in the lightly whipped cream. Spoon into small cocotte dishes. Chill for 3–4 hours. Serve with fingers of toast or brown bread and butter.

The mousse can be extended by adding grated cheese; 3 oz added to the above ingredients would make sufficient mousse for 6.

(American: $\frac{1}{2}$ cup cream cheese, $\frac{1}{2}$ cup double cream)

Carrot and raisin salad

Serves 4
4 large carrots, peeled and grated
2 oz seedless raisins
juice and grated rind of 1 orange
2 teasp sugar
4 tbsp olive oil
seasoning

Mix the grated carrot with the raisins. Blend the orange juice with the grated orange rind, sugar, oil and seasoning. Stir into the carrot and raisins. Chill well before serving.

To turn the salad into a 'starter', add a little chopped ham, a few peeled prawns, or a little flaked cooked fish.

(American: $\frac{1}{4}$ cup raisins)

Carrots with aioli

Serves 4
1 lb carrots: either large carrots, peeled and cut into strips, or young whole carrots
salt
ground black pepper
sprigs of watercress
3 cloves crushed garlic
good pinch sugar
$\frac{1}{4}$ pint olive oil
2 tbsp chopped parsley
juice $\frac{1}{2}$ lemon

Sprinkle the carrot strips or young whole carrots with salt and pepper, and mix with the watercress.

For the aioli: mix the crushed garlic with the sugar, oil and parsley, to give a thick dressing. Add lemon juice to taste. Serve aioli as a separate 'dip sauce' with the carrots. This dressing will keep in the refrigerator for up to 2 weeks, but keep the container well covered as the flavour will quickly spread to other foods.

(American: 3 cups carrot strips or whole young carrots, $\frac{1}{2}$ cup olive oil)

Braised carrots

Serves 4
1 onion
1 lb carrots, peeled and cut into lengthways slices
bay leaf
2 tbsp chopped parsley
seasoning
1 teasp sugar
$\frac{1}{4}$ pint chicken stock
$\frac{1}{4}$ pint brown ale

Put the sliced onion into the base of a small casserole. Add the sliced carrots, bay leaf, chopped parsley, seasoning, sugar, stock and ale. Cover the casserole with a lid. Cook at Mark 4, 350°F, for 45–50 minutes. Check that the liquid does not evaporate and the casserole become too dry.

(American: 3 cups sliced carrot, $\frac{1}{2}$ cup stock, $\frac{1}{2}$ cup ale)

Fried carrots with croutons

Serves 4
$\frac{1}{2}$ lb carrots
oil
2 slices bread
seasoning

Peel and slice the carrots. Put into a pan and add sufficient boiling water to just cover. Bring back to the boil and simmer for 5 minutes. Drain carrots. Remove crusts from bread and cut into even-sized cubes. Fry the bread cubes in hot oil until pale straw in colour. Drain on absorbent paper. Add carrots to the oil remaining in the pan, and cook for 4–5 minutes. Return croutons to the pan, and toss together for 2–3 minutes. Drain well before serving. Season to taste.

(American: $1\frac{1}{2}$ cups sliced carrots)

Fried carrots julienne

Serves 4
4 large carrots
celery salt
ground black pepper
2 oz butter
1 teasp sugar

Peel the carrots. Using a very sharp knife, cut them into small, thin strips the size of a matchstick. Soak in $\frac{1}{2}$ pint iced water for 1 hour—this will crisp the matchstick strips of carrot, but not destroy the vitamin C content. Drain the carrot strips thoroughly. Sprinkle with celery salt and pepper. Melt butter in a pan. Add the strips of carrot and toss over a moderate heat until lightly tender, but still crisp. Stir in the sugar and serve immediately.

Celery is just as good cooked in the same way.

(American: 1 cup iced water, $\frac{1}{4}$ cup butter)

Carrots lyonnaise

Serves 4
This is one of the simplest and most delicious ways of cooking carrots; dry cider can be used in place of white wine.

1 lb carrots, peeled and sliced
$\frac{1}{2}$ pint white wine
1 large onion, sliced
2 oz butter
seasoning
juice $\frac{1}{2}$ lemon

Put the sliced carrots into a shallow pan with the wine, onion, butter, seasoning and lemon juice. Cover the pan with a lid or a circle of greased foil. Bring to the boil and simmer very gently for 35–40 minutes, until the carrots are just tender. Some of the liquid will evaporate during cooking.

(American: 3 cups sliced carrot, 1 cup wine, $\frac{1}{4}$ cup butter)

Sweet carrots

Serves 4
Carrots are naturally sweet, and the addition of honey helps to bring out their full flavour.
1 lb small young carrots
$\frac{1}{4}$ pint chicken stock
$1\frac{1}{2}$ oz butter
3 tbsp clear honey
pinch mixed spice
seasoning

Scrub the carrots thoroughly, but do not peel them. Put the whole carrots into a pan with the stock, butter, honey, mixed spice and seasoning. Cover the pan with a lid or a greased circle of foil. Bring to the boil. Simmer gently, until the carrots are just tender.

The carrots can also be cooked inside the oven. Put them into a casserole with the other ingredients. Cook at 350°F, Mark 4, for about 45 minutes.

(American: 3 cups whole small carrots, $\frac{1}{2}$ cup chicken stock, 3 tbsp butter)

Carrots in cream

Serves 4
1 lb large carrots
2 oz butter
1 onion
$\frac{1}{4}$ pint cream (see recipe)
1 egg yolk
seasoning

Peel the carrots. Cut into thin slices. Layer the sliced carrots in a greased ovenproof dish, with the butter and the finely chopped onion. Beat the cream with the egg yolk and the seasoning. Spoon evenly over the carrots. Cover the dish with a piece of greased foil or greaseproof paper. Cook at 350°F, Mark 4, for about 45 minutes.

Single, double or soured cream can be used in this recipe. With thin cream, the final cooking liquid will be much thinner.

(American: 3 cups sliced carrot, $\frac{1}{4}$ cup butter, $\frac{1}{2}$ cup cream)

Cheese and chive carrots

Serves 4
1 lb large carrots
3 oz cream cheese
seasoning
2 tbsp chopped chives

Peel the carrots. Cut into small cubes with a sharp knife. Put into a pan and add sufficient water to just cover the base of the pan. Cover with a lid. Simmer the carrots until they are just tender. Most of the liquid will have evaporated, but drain off any excess. Return the hot diced carrots to the pan. Add the cream cheese, cut into small cubes, the seasoning and chives. Heat through over a moderate heat, until the cheese melts, and forms a sauce.

If chives are difficult to obtain, use chopped parsley instead.

(American: 3 cups cubed carrot, $\frac{1}{2}$ cup cream cheese)

Pureed carrots

Serves 4–6
This is one way of getting children, who would otherwise refuse, to eat carrots.

$1\frac{1}{2}$ lb large carrots
juice $\frac{1}{2}$ orange
seasoning
1 oz butter
4 tbsp cream
1 oz crisp golden breadcrumbs

Peel and slice the carrots. Put into a pan with $\frac{1}{4}$ pint water or chicken stock. Cover the pan and bring to the boil. Simmer until carrots are just tender. Drain the carrots, reserving the cooking liquid. Mash the carrots with a potato masher, push through a sieve, or blend in a liquidizer, to give a smooth puree. Beat in the orange juice, seasoning, butter and cream. Thin with a little of the reserved cooking liquid if the puree is too thick. Return the carrot puree to a pan, and heat through over a gentle heat. Spoon into a serving dish and sprinkle with the crumbs.

(American: 4 cups sliced carrot, $\frac{1}{2}$ cup water or stock, 2 tbsp butter, 2 tbsp breadcrumbs)

Carrot fritters

Serves 4
4 oz plain flour
pinch salt
pinch powdered mustard
1 egg
$\frac{1}{3}$ pint milk
$\frac{1}{2}$ lb large carrots
seasoning
oil
soured cream

Sieve the flour and salt into a bowl. Add the mustard, egg and a little milk. Beat to a smooth paste. Gradually beat in the remaining milk. Peel the carrots and grate coarsely. Mix the grated carrot into the batter. Grease the base of a solid frying pan or a griddle with oil. Drop spoonfuls of the carrot batter on to the oiled surface, and cook over a moderate heat, until the underside is set and golden. Flip the fritters over, and cook on the other side until golden. Sprinkle with seasoning to taste. Serve immediately, topped with soured cream.

(American: 1 cup plain flour, $\frac{2}{3}$ cup milk, $\frac{3}{4}$ cup grated carrot)

Carrot dumplings

Serves 4
8 oz plain flour
seasoning
grated rind $\frac{1}{2}$ orange

4 oz shredded suet
3 large carrots
1 beaten egg
chicken stock

Sieve the flour and seasoning into a
bowl. Add the grated orange rind,
and the suet. Peel the carrots and
grate coarsely. Add the grated carrot
to the dry ingredients, and bind
together with the beaten egg. Form
the mixture into 8 even-sized balls,
with floured hands. Put about 1 pint
chicken stock into a pan and bring
to the boil. Carefully drop in the
dumplings and cook gently for 20
minutes; the dumplings should
swell slightly, and rise to the surface.
Serve very hot, topped with melted
butter.

(American: 2 cups plain flour, 1 cup
shredded suet, 2 cups chicken stock)

Cover pan. Bring to the boil and
simmer for 8 minutes.

Meanwhile, make the sauce: melt
the butter in a pan. Add the flour
and cook for 1 minute. Gradually
stir in the stock and milk. Bring to
the boil and stir over the heat until
thickened. Season to taste. Add the
drained carrots and the chopped hard
boiled egg. Spoon into a greased
overproof dish. Sprinkle the surface
with the crumbs and grated cheese.
Bake at 375°F, Mark 5, for 30
minutes.

(American: 3 cups sliced carrot,
3 tbsp butter, 3 tbsp flour, $\frac{1}{2}$ cup
chicken stock, $\frac{1}{2}$ cup milk, $1\frac{1}{2}$ tbsp
grated cheese)

*Carrot and egg pie

Serves 4–6
1 lb carrots
$1\frac{1}{2}$ oz butter
$1\frac{1}{2}$ oz flour
$\frac{1}{4}$ pint chicken stock
$\frac{1}{4}$ pint milk
seasoning
4 hard boiled eggs
3 tbsp breadcrumbs
$1\frac{1}{2}$ oz grated cheese

Peel the carrots and cut into slices.
Put into a pan with $\frac{1}{4}$ pint water.

Mushrooms

Mushrooms are among the most
versatile of vegetables. Both wild and
cultivated mushrooms can turn a
simple dish into something quite
special. Julius Caesar described
mushrooms as 'the food of gods',
and he reserved all that he could find
for himself and his men. Mushrooms
have come a long way since then, and
have lost their battle against
cultivation. They were first cultivated
in France, at the end of the
seventeenth century. They were then
considered to be a delicacy for the
privileged few, and only gained real
popularity at the end of the Second
World War.

The three principal grades of cultivated mushrooms are
button: tiny, firm-closed and white;
cup: the button which has begun to grow and open up, showing the pinkish gills;
flat or open: fully-opened and mature in flavour, and much darker in colour.

Cultivation has both increased the supply of mushrooms and made them obtainable all the year round. Though wild mushrooms can still be found, they are rarely obtainable in shops, and unless you have some expert knowledge of edible fungi, it is inadvisable to hunt for your own. There are many poisonous varieties which closely resemble edible fungi.

Open mushrooms deteriorate quite quickly and need using within one to two days of purchase, whereas cup and button mushrooms, if in peak condition, can be kept for up to a week in a cool, dry place.

Raw mushrooms are ideal for slimmers. They contain only two calories per ounce, and though they have little or no actual food value, they can be made into delicious snacks and salads.

There is little or no wastage with cultivated mushrooms; the whole mushroom, including the skin, can be eaten. For successful results when cooking them, you should use the right variety to suit the recipe. Open mushrooms, without doubt, are the best for grilling, as part of a mixed grill or with bacon, whereas cup and button mushrooms are more suitable for casseroles, pies, soups and salads. Whichever type you are using, it is important not to overcook them. Mushrooms have a delicate flavour and texture, which can easily be spoilt. Mushrooms are done if they give slightly when pierced with a fork. Always add mushrooms to a dish that requires prolonged cooking time, such as a casserole, towards the end of the cooking. Cook mushrooms as an accompanying vegetable in the following ways.

For button and cup mushrooms: melt 2 oz butter in a pan and add 6 oz of washed and dried mushrooms, seasoning, pinch of powdered nutmeg, 1 tbsp stock and a piece of lemon peel. Cover the pan and cook for 4–5 minutes (American: $\frac{1}{4}$ cup butter, $1\frac{1}{2}$ cups mushrooms).

For flat mushrooms: wash and dry 6 oz mushrooms (American: $1\frac{1}{2}$ cups). Remove the stalks. Put them into a shallow dish and add 5 tbsp oil or melted butter, and seasoning. Leave the mushrooms to stand for one hour. Put them into a grill pan, cups uppermost, and spoon over some of the fat. Grill for 2 minutes. Turn the mushrooms, spoon over the fat, and grill for a further 2 minutes.

Mushroom salad

Serves 4

6 oz button or cup mushrooms
small bunch spring onions
4 tbsp mayonnaise (see p 15)
1 teasp dill seeds
juice 1 lemon
seasoning
2 rashers crispy fried bacon

Wipe the mushrooms and cut into slices. Chop the spring onions, discarding the root ends, and mix with the sliced mushrooms. Blend the mayonnaise with the dill seed, lemon juice and seasoning and add a little sugar if liked. Stir into the mushrooms and onion. Sprinkle the salad with the chopped crispy bacon. For an extra tangy dressing, stir in a little creamed horseradish.

(American: $1\frac{1}{2}$ cups sliced mushrooms)

Mushroom and rice cocktails

Serves 4

2 oz long grain rice
chicken stock
4 oz button or cup mushrooms
6 tbsp vinaigrette (see below)
seasoning
4 tbsp soured cream
2 oz peeled prawns
cayenne pepper

Put rice into a pan with about $\frac{1}{3}$ pint chicken stock. Bring to the boil and simmer until the rice is tender. Drain thoroughly. Wipe and slice the mushrooms. Toss in the vinaigrette dressing. Stir into the warm rice. Chill. Spoon the rice mixture into stemmed glasses. Top with soured cream and prawns, and sprinkle with cayenne pepper. Serve with rye or brown bread.

For the vinaigrette: mix 4 tbsp oil (preferably olive) with 2 tbsp white wine vinegar, 2 teasp mustard, a pinch of sugar and seasoning. The vinaigrette can be made up in larger quantities, and stored in a corked bottle in a cool place, for up to 2 weeks.

(American: $\frac{1}{4}$ cup long grain rice, 1 cup button mushrooms, $\frac{1}{2}$ cup peeled prawns)

*Potted mushrooms

Serves 4

6 oz button or cup mushrooms
1 clove crushed garlic
6 oz butter
grated rind $\frac{1}{2}$ lemon
seasoning

Coarsely chop the wiped mushrooms. Fry the crushed garlic in half the butter for 1 minute. Add the chopped mushrooms and continue frying for a further 3 minutes. Drain the mushrooms with a perforated spoon, or through a sieve. Put the drained mushrooms into 4 individual dishes.

Add remaining butter, the lemon rind and seasoning to the cooking butter in the pan. Heat until melted and pour over the mushrooms. Cool. Chill to set. Serve with thin fingers of hot toast.

(American: $1\frac{1}{2}$ cups chopped mushrooms, $\frac{3}{4}$ cup butter)

Souffle mushrooms

Serves 4
6 oz open mushrooms
2 oz butter
pinch nutmeg
seasoning
2 eggs
4 tbsp double cream
a little grated Parmesan cheese

Peel the mushrooms and chop roughly. Melt butter, add chopped mushrooms and fry until just tender. Stir in the seasoning, egg yolks and cream. Carefully fold in the stiffly beaten egg whites. Spoon into 4 greased individual ovenproof dishes. Sprinkle with grated Parmesan cheese. Bake at 375°F, Mark 5, for about 25 minutes, until puffed and golden.

(American: $1\frac{1}{2}$ cups chopped mushrooms, $\frac{1}{4}$ cup butter)

Mushrooms a la francaise

Serves 4
$\frac{1}{2}$ lettuce
2 oz butter
seasoning
$\frac{1}{4}$ lb button or cup mushrooms

Wash the lettuce. Shred coarsely. Arrange a layer of shredded lettuce in the base of a greased ovenproof casserole, using about half the lettuce. Season, and top with small knobs of butter. Add the sliced mushrooms. Top with the remaining lettuce and butter. Cover with a lid or piece of buttered foil. Cook at 350°F, Mark 4, for about 40 minutes.

(American: $\frac{1}{4}$ cup butter, 1 cup sliced mushrooms)

*Mushrooms a la grecque

Serves 4
1 onion
1 clove crushed garlic
$\frac{1}{4}$ pint oil
3 tbsp white wine vinegar
little chopped tarragon
2 tbsp chopped parsley
bay leaf
6 oz button or cup mushrooms

Fry the finely chopped onion and the crushed garlic gently in 3 tbsp oil for 4 minutes. Add the remaining oil, wine vinegar and herbs. Simmer gently for 20 minutes. Add the whole mushrooms, and simmer gently until the mushrooms are just tender. It is important not to overcook them. Cool and then chill—for a minimum of 2 hours. Serve with crusty bread. These mushrooms can be served hot, if preferred, but the flavours mingle better when served cold.

(American: generous $\frac{1}{2}$ cup oil, $1\frac{1}{2}$ cups button or cup mushrooms)

Mushrooms with black butter sauce

Serves 4
$\frac{1}{4}$ lb open, button or cup mushrooms
3 oz butter
salt
$1\frac{1}{2}$ teasp crushed peppercorns
juice $\frac{1}{2}$ lemon

If using open mushrooms, peel them and cut into thick slices. For button or cup mushrooms, wipe and leave whole. Melt 2 oz of the butter with salt and crushed peppercorns. Add the mushrooms. Fry gently until mushrooms are just tender. Remove mushrooms to a hot serving dish and keep warm. Add remaining butter to the pan and heat until it begins to turn nutty brown. Add the lemon juice and heat until bubbling. Pour over the mushrooms and serve.

(American: 1 cup mushrooms, $\frac{1}{3}$ cup butter)

Deep fried mushrooms

Serves 4
$\frac{1}{2}$ lb button or cup mushrooms
seasoned flour
3 oz plain flour
seasoning
1 egg
$\frac{1}{4}$ pint milk
1 large clove crushed garlic
oil for deep frying

Dust the mushrooms with the seasoned flour, shaking off any excess. Sieve the flour and seasoning, and mix to a smooth paste with the egg and a little of the milk. Gradually beat in the remaining milk. Add the crushed garlic. Dip the mushrooms in the batter, to give an even coating, and then carefully drop into hot deep fat. Fry until crisp and golden. Drain well on absorbent paper. Serve piping hot with tartare sauce.

For the tartare sauce: mix 5 tbsp mayonnaise (see p 15) with 2 tbsp capers, 1 tbsp chopped gherkin and seasoning.

(American: 2 cups button or cup mushrooms, 6 tbsp plain flour, $\frac{1}{2}$ cup milk)

Brandied mushrooms

Serves 4
6 oz button or cup mushrooms
1 small onion
1 clove crushed garlic

2 oz butter
3 tbsp brandy
seasoning

Wipe and halve the mushrooms. Chop the onion finely. Fry the chopped onion and the crushed garlic in the melted butter for 4 minutes. Add the halved mushrooms and seasoning. Cover the pan and cook gently for about 5 minutes; the mushrooms should still be slightly firm. Add the brandy and heat through. Carefully put a lighted match or taper to the surface of the liquid, to set it alight. Allow the flames to die down, then serve immediately.

The mushrooms can either be served as a vegetable with grilled meats or fish, or as an appetizer with fingers of toast or crusty bread.

(American: $1\frac{1}{2}$ cups button or cup mushrooms, $\frac{1}{4}$ cup butter)

Tipsy mushrooms

Serves 4
6 oz mushrooms, either whole button or cup, or sliced open ones
2 oz butter
2 rashers bacon
seasoning
$\frac{1}{4}$ pint brown ale
$\frac{1}{2}$ tbsp flour

Put the mushrooms into a pan with the melted butter and the chopped bacon. Fry gently for 3 minutes. Add the seasoning and brown ale. Bring to the boil, and simmer gently for 5 minutes. Blend the flour with a little cold water. Add to the mushrooms, and stir over a gentle heat until the sauce thickens. Sprinkle with chopped parsley and serve immediately with crusty bread which has been warmed through in the oven.

(American: $1\frac{1}{2}$ cups mushrooms, $\frac{1}{4}$ cup butter, generous $\frac{1}{2}$ cup ale)

*Stroganoff mushrooms

Serves 4
small can tuna fish
can anchovy fillets
1 tbsp capers
$\frac{1}{4}$ pint mayonnaise (see p 15)
juice $\frac{1}{2}$ lemon
seasoning
6 oz button mushrooms
5 tbsp vinaigrette (see p 32)

If you have a liquidizer, blend the tuna fish with the anchovy fillets (reserving a few for garnish), capers, mayonnaise, lemon juice and seasoning. Alternatively, pound the ingredients together in a bowl with a wooden spoon until well mixed. This gives a coarser textured sauce, but it is just as good. Wipe the mushrooms and toss them in the vinaigrette. Put into 4 individual shallow dishes.

Spoon the tuna sauce evenly over the top. Decorate with the remaining anchovy fillets.

(American: ⅓ cup canned tuna fish, 2 tbsp anchovy fillets, a generous ½ cup mayonnaise, 1½ cups button mushrooms)

*Mushroom puffs

Serves 4
20 button or cup mushrooms
3 oz pate
2 oz softened butter
1 large clove crushed garlic
seasoning
6 oz puff pastry
beaten egg
oil for deep frying
parsley

Remove the stalks from the wiped mushrooms. Mix the softened butter with the crushed garlic and seasoning. Put a little flavoured butter into the cap of each mushroom, and then top with a little pate. Roll the puff pastry out thinly. Cut into small circles, using a 2½ in– 3 in fluted pastry cutter. Brush the pastry edges with beaten egg. Put a mushroom in the centre of each pastry circle. Pull up the pastry edges, and pinch together to seal. Chill for 1 hour. Lower the pastry covered mushrooms into a pan of hot deep fat. Deep fry until well puffed and golden. Drain. Serve

immediately, garnished with parsley and a herb sauce.

For the herb sauce: mix ¼ pint soured cream with the grated rind ½ lemon, 1 teasp dill seed, 1½ teasp chopped tarragon and seasoning. *Freeze the mushroom puffs before deep frying*

(American: ⅓ cup pate, ¼ cup butter, approx 1 cup pastry, ½ cup soured cream)

Mushroom scramble

Serves 4
1½ oz butter
4 oz button or cup mushrooms
4 eggs
seasoning
2 tbsp cream
2 slices toast
butter
1½ oz grated cheese

Melt the butter. Add the sliced wiped mushrooms. Fry gently for 3 minutes. Beat the eggs with the seasoning and cream. Add to the fried mushrooms. Stir over a gentle heat until the mixture scrambles; it should still be quite soft. Put into a greased ovenproof dish. Spread the toast generously with butter, and cut into triangles. Arrange on top of the mushroom scramble. Sprinkle the top with grated cheese. Put under a moderate grill until the cheese melts and turns golden. Do not grill for too long, until the egg becomes solid and dry.

(American: 3 tbsp butter, 1 cup sliced mushrooms, 3 tbsp grated cheese)

Mushroom rarebits

Serves 4
16 open mushrooms
8 rashers bacon
French mustard
4 slices white bread
6 oz grated cheese

Peel the mushrooms, and trim the stalks if they are very long. Remove the rinds from the bacon and cut each rasher in half. Spread one side evenly with mustard. Wrap each piece of bacon around a mushroom. Toast the bread on one side only. Spread the untoasted side generously with butter. Arrange four mushroom and bacon rolls on the buttered side of each piece of bread. Put under a moderate grill for 4–5 minutes. Top generously with grated cheese. Return to the grill, until the cheese bubbles and turns golden.

(American: $1\frac{1}{2}$ cups grated cheese)

*Stuffed mushrooms

Serves 4
12 large open mushrooms
1 small onion
$1\frac{1}{2}$ oz butter

2 tbsp oil
5 oz cooked salmon, or other fresh or canned fish
2 oz fresh breadcrumbs
1 egg
seasoning

Peel the mushrooms, and remove the stalks. Chop the mushroom stalks and chop the onion finely. Fry the chopped onion in butter and oil for 4 minutes. Add the chopped mushroom stalks, and fry for a further 3 minutes. Mix with the cooked fish, breadcrumbs, beaten egg and seasoning. Spoon the stuffing into the caps of the mushrooms. Stand the mushrooms in a shallow ovenproof dish. Dribble with a little oil or melted butter. Bake at 375°F, Mark 5, for 20–25 minutes.

The mushrooms can be prepared the night before, and refrigerated. They are ready for cooking when needed.

(American: 3 tbsp butter, a generous cup cooked or canned fish, $\frac{1}{2}$ cup fresh breadcrumbs)

Onions

The onion is one of the oldest known vegetables. It was used during the times of the pharaohs, and it is listed in the records of the slaves who built the Great Pyramid at Giza. It was introduced into Europe during the sixteenth century by Spanish explorers, who returned with the seeds from the Far East, and from that time has been popular in every European cuisine. It is difficult to imagine cooking without onions today: they are an integral ingredient in so many savoury dishes. The three most familiar types of onion are

Spanish: a large onion, with a shiny brown skin; the English equivalent tends to be smaller, and has a variegated skin.

Button: a small, compact onion, which is normally used whole rather than chopped; the shallot, with a slightly purplish tinge to the skin, is a member of the same family, and is used mainly for pickling.

Spring: this has a small bulb and a spindly green stem. It is used mainly in salads. The stem can be chopped and used in place of chives for cooking or as a garnish.

Spring onions and shallots are both available during springtime. The other types of onion are generally available all the year.

Onions keep extremely well unless they have been attacked by frost, when their skins tend to shrivel and discolour. Store them in a cool, dry, dark place. They will remain fresh for about two weeks. Onions have a very strong, pungent flavour, so keep them well away from foods with a more subtle flavour. Cover dishes in the refrigerator that contain onion. This prevents the flavour from spreading to other more bland foods such as butter and milk.

Onions have little nutritional value of their own. It is still believed, however, that the strong, pungent smell is beneficial to those suffering from colds and other respiratory complaints.

Prepare onion according to your recipe: if it is to be fried quickly, or cooked for only a short time, chop it finely; if, however, it is to be used in a stew or casserole, or in a dish that is cooked for a fairly long time, slice it or chop it roughly. Onion browns very quickly when fried in butter or oil, so to retain its colour, fry it gently. This is often called 'sweating', and is best done in a covered pan. Grate the onion coarsely for quick cooking onion, when you need only the flavour and not the texture. When stuffing or roasting whole onions, first blanch them for a few minutes in boiling water, so that they will cook more rapidly and thoroughly.

*French onion soup

Serves 4–6
3 large onions
2 oz bacon fat or dripping
1 pint beef stock
$\frac{1}{8}$ pint red wine
seasoning
slices of stale French bread
grated cheese

Slice the onions evenly. Melt the fat and add the sliced onion. Fry the onion for 5 minutes. Add the beef stock, red wine and seasoning. Bring to the boil. Cover the pan and simmer for 25–30 minutes.

Sprinkle the slices of stale bread with an even layer of cheese. Put under a moderate grill, until the cheese starts to bubble. Float the cheese croutes on top of the soup before serving.

Freeze without the croutes

(American: ¼ cup bacon fat or dripping, 2½ cups beef stock, generous ¼ cup red wine)

Onion and gruyere salad

Serves 4
2 large onions
¼ lb gruyere cheese
2 tbsp chopped parsley
juice and grated rind 1 orange
⅛ pint oil
pinch sugar
seasoning

Cut the peeled onions into rings. Cut the cheese into thin slivers; if you have a solid block of cheese, you can do this either with a cheese slice or with a potato peeler. Mix the onion rings with the slivers of cheese and the chopped parsley. Blend the orange juice and grated rind with the oil, sugar and seasoning for the dressing. Pour over the onion and cheese and toss lightly together.

(American: generous ¼ cup oil)

*Onion cheese

Serves 4
2 medium size onions

1 clove crushed garlic
seasoning
1 tbsp chopped parsley
6 oz cottage cheese

Peel the onions and grate them coarsely. Drain on absorbent paper, to remove any excess moisture. Mix the grated onion with the crushed garlic, seasoning, chopped parsley, and the sieved cottage cheese. Press into a pot and chill, covered with a layer of foil or cling wrap. Serve with fingers of hot toast, or as a filling for baked jacket potatoes.

(American: 1 cup cottage cheese)

Mimosa onions

Serves 6
6 medium size onions
chicken stock
seasoning
⅛ pint mayonnaise (see p 15)
2 hard boiled eggs
chopped parsley

Peel the onions and put into a pan with sufficient stock to just cover. Bring to the boil. Cover the pan and simmer until tender. Test the onions by piercing with a cocktail stick. Mix the mayonnaise with the chopped hard boiled egg white. Put the drained onions into an ovenproof dish and spoon the mayonnaise over the top. Put under a hot grill to glaze the surface of the sauce. Sprinkle the top with the sieved hard boiled egg yolk and parsley.

(American: generous $\frac{1}{4}$ cup mayonnaise)

Crispy fried onions

Serves 4
2 large onions
milk
seasoned flour
fat for deep frying

Cut the peeled onions into rings, about $\frac{1}{4}$ in thick. Dip the onion rings into milk, and then into seasoned flour to give an even coating. Carefully drop into hot deep fat and fry until golden brown and crisp. Drain well. Serve with grilled meats, or as an accompaniment to drinks. The crispy onions make a pleasant change from crisps and nuts.

Onions with parsley butter

Serves 4
$\frac{3}{4}$ lb button onions
$\frac{1}{2}$ pint white wine
seasoning
bay leaf
3 oz butter
3 tbsp chopped parsley
1 clove crushed garlic

Peel the onions and put into a shallow pan. Add the white wine

seasoning and bay leaf. Cover the pan and simmer until the onions are just tender. Top with small knobs of garlic and parsley butter, just before serving.

For the parsley butter: cream the butter until soft. Mix with the chopped parsley and the crushed garlic. Wrap in a piece of foil or greased paper and chill until firm.

This butter can be made in larger quantities, for topping steaks, fish cutlets, etc.

(American: 3 cups button onions, 6 tbsp butter, $1\frac{1}{4}$ cups white wine)

Onions in soured cream

Serves 4
2 large onions
2 oz butter
seasoning
$\frac{1}{4}$ pint soured cream

Peel the onions and cut into thick slices. Fry gently in the melted butter, until the onions are almost tender. Season to taste. Stir in the soured cream. Heat the onions through in their cream sauce.

Variation: sprinkle the onions with a thick layer of grated cheese, and pop under a hot grill, until the cheese melts and turns golden brown.

(American: $\frac{1}{4}$ cup butter, generous $\frac{1}{2}$ cup soured cream)

*Onions almondine

Serves 4
2 large onions
2 oz butter
1 tbsp oil
seasoning
3 tbsp clear honey
1½ oz split almonds

Peel and slice the onions. Melt the butter and oil. Add the sliced onions and fry until lightly golden—about 7–8 minutes. Add the seasoning, honey and split almonds. Simmer for 5 minutes.

Onions almondine are particularly delicious spooned over sliced boiled bacon or grilled gammon steaks.

(American: ¼ cup butter, ¼ cup split almonds)

Onion sambal

Serves 4–6
2 onions
1 clove crushed garlic
1 tbsp chopped fresh mint (or 1 teasp dried mint)
¼ pint natural yogurt
1 teasp chilli paste
few drops Tabasco
seasoning
1 teasp sugar

Peel and slice the onions. Mix the crushed garlic with the chopped mint, natural yogurt, chilli paste, Tabasco, seasoning and sugar. Spoon over the sliced onion, and mix well together. Serve with curries and other hot spicy dishes.

The sambal will keep well in a covered dish in the refrigerator, for 2–3 days.

(American: generous ½ cup natural yogurt)

*Onions monaguesque

Serves 4
¾ lb button onions
14 oz can tomatoes
2 teasp brown sugar
2 oz raisins
1 clove crushed garlic
1 tbsp tomato puree
seasoning

Peel the button onions and put into a pan. Add all the remaining ingredients. Simmer until the onions are tender and glossy, and the sauce has reduced.

The onions can be served hot, but they are particularly delicious cold.

(American: 3 cups button onions, 1½ cups canned tomatoes, ¼ cup raisins)

*Oriental onions

Serves 4
¾ lb button onions
2 tbsp oil
1 oz butter

small can crushed pineapple (or two thick slices of fresh pineapple, chopped finely)
1 red pepper
1 tbsp vinegar
juice $\frac{1}{2}$ lemon
1 tbsp brown sugar
pinch ground ginger
seasoning

Peel the onions. Melt the butter and oil in a pan and add the peeled onions. Fry gently until lightly golden. Put the remaining ingredients into a separate pan, and simmer for 10 minutes. Pour over the onions, and continue simmering until the onions are just tender.

These are equally good served hot or cold.

(American: 3 cups button onions, 2 tbsp butter, 1 cup canned crushed pineapple)

Devilled onion kebabs

Serves 4
3 tbsp oil
1 tbsp curry powder
2 teasp Worcestershire sauce
1 teasp mustard
seasoning
20 button onions

Mix the oil, curry powder, Worcestershire sauce, mustard and seasoning. Peel the button onions. Put into a pan with sufficient boiling water to just cover. Bring back to the boil and simmer for 5 minutes. Drain well. Thread the onions onto skewers—5 on each. Spoon the devilled baste over the onions. Put under a moderate grill, and grill for 4–5 minutes. Turn the skewers, and grill for a further 4–5 minutes, glazing once more with the devilled baste.

Serve with grilled or cold meats, or as an appetizer by themselves.

(American: any brown sauce in place of Worcestershire sauce)

*Onion ragout

Serves 4–6
3 large onions
1 clove crushed garlic
3 tbsp oil
1 teasp chopped basil
3 large ripe tomatoes
$\frac{1}{4}$ pint chicken stock

Chop the peeled onions coarsely. Fry the chopped onion and the crushed garlic in the oil for 5 minutes together with the chopped basil. Plunge the tomatoes into boiling water for a few seconds. Remove the skins, and chop the tomato flesh. Add to the onion with the stock. Simmer gently for 20 minutes. Serve as a sauce.

(American: generous $\frac{1}{2}$ cup chicken stock)

*Onion gratin

Serves 4
2 large onions
2 tbsp oil
1 oz butter
seasoning
2 oz grated cheese
1 oz breadcrumbs

Peel and slice the onions. Melt the butter and oil. Add the sliced onion and fry gently until soft. Put the fried onion into a greased shallow ovenproof dish. Add the seasoning to taste. Sprinkle with grated cheese and the breadcrumbs. Bake at 375°F, Mark 5, for 20–25 minutes.

(American: 2 tbsp butter, ⅓ cup grated cheese, 2 tbsp breadcrumbs)

*Onion quiche

Serves 4–6
6 oz shortcrust pastry
3 onions
1 clove crushed garlic
3 tbsp oil
1 oz butter
¼ pint cream
2 eggs
seasoning
1 oz grated Parmesan cheese

Roll out the pastry, and use to line a 7½ in–8 in flan tin. Trim the edges and prick the base. Peel and slice the onions. Melt the butter and oil. Add the sliced onion and garlic, and fry gently for 5 minutes. Spoon into the pastry case. Beat the cream with the eggs and seasoning and pour into the pastry case. Sprinkle the top with Parmesan cheese. Bake at 375°F, Mark 5, for about 40 minutes.

(American: approx. 1 cup pastry, 2 tbsp butter, generous ½ cup cream, 2 tbsp grated Parmesan cheese)

Roast stuffed onions

Serves 4
4 large onions
1 oz butter
5 tbsp oil
4 oz pork sausagemeat, or chopped
    cooked pork
1 teasp mixed herbs
seasoning
1 oz breadcrumbs
1 egg yolk

Peel the onions, and carefully hollow out the centres. Parboil the onions for 6 minutes. Drain well. Chop the centre onion quite finely. Melt the butter and 1 tbsp of the oil. Add the chopped onion and fry until soft. Mix with the sausagemeat, herbs, seasoning, crumbs and egg yolk. Press the meat stuffing into the centres of the onions. Put onions into a greased ovenproof dish and spoon over the remaining oil. Bake at 375°F, Mark 5, for 40–45 minutes.

(American: 2 tbsp butter, 1 cup sausagemeat, 2 tbsp breadcrumbs)

Potatoes

Today potatoes are part of the staple British diet, and it would be difficult for many of us to imagine a meal without the well-loved 'spud'. On average, the British eat in excess of 200 lbs of potatoes per head, per year.

Yet, if Sir Walter Raleigh hadn't brought back the potato from America, at the beginning of the sixteenth century, we might never have sampled a jacket potato, chips, or a plate of mash.

Potatoes have been grown commercially in this country, since the beginning of the eighteenth century. There are many different varieties, but, for culinary purposes, it is sufficient to divide them into two categories

old: most old potatoes available in Britain are good all-rounders, and properly cooked will give satisfactory results, whether boiled, mashed, baked, roasted or chipped. Some varieties are, however, slightly better suited than others to various cooking methods. Majestics are excellent for roasting and baking, Pentland Ivory for chipping or sauteeing; and King Edward for boiling or mashing.

New: there is less differentiation among new potatoes. They are usually boiled, and for that method Jersey, Arran Pilot, Home Guard or Epicure are equally suitable.

Old potatoes are at their best from September until April. The new potato season complements that of the old: it is from May until August.

Potatoes keep very well. If you use 7 lb or more per week, it is economical to buy them in bulk. Most greengrocers will supply them by the sack, and there are also potato farmers in rural areas, offering special delivery services.

Always store potatoes in a cool, dry, dark place; damp causes rot and excess warmth makes them sprout. Potatoes taint very easily, so keep them away from strong smelling foods, or commodities such as paraffin.

Potatoes comprise a good balance of nutrients; they contain vitamins B and C, iron and calcium, and a small amount of protein. Their calorific value is high, so slimmers should only occasionally eat a small portion.

The two simple methods of cooking potatoes are boiling and baking. To boil old potatoes, peel them thinly: most of the vitamin C content lies just beneath the skin. If potatoes are very large, cut them into small pieces of the same size, so that they cook evenly. Put the potatoes into a pan with a generous pinch of salt and sufficient cold water to just cover them. Add a little lemon juice or wine vinegar to the water to prevent the potatoes discolouring. Bring the water to the boil. Cover the pan, and simmer the potatoes until they are just tender. Drain thoroughly. The potatoes are now ready to be served as they are, or to be mashed with butter and milk or a little cream. Use the drained potato water for gravies or soups.

To boil new potatoes, just scrub them and cook them in their skins— the skin on a new potato is not tough. Put them into a pan with a good pinch of salt. Add water to a depth of 1 in, a generous knob of butter, and a sprig of mint or a little mint jelly. Bring the water to the boil. Cover the pan and simmer the potatoes until they are just tender. Drain, and toss the potatoes in a little extra butter and a generous pinch of ground nutmeg.

To bake potatoes in their jackets: Select even-sized potatoes, free from blemishes and large 'eyes'. Scrub them well so that the skins are scrupulously clean. Prick at regular intervals with a skewer; this ensures that they cook evenly, right through to the centre. Rub the skins with a little oil and salt to help crisp the skin during baking. Bake in a hot oven, 425°F, Mark 7, for about 1½ hours (the baking time depends to a certain extent on the size of the potato). Split the tops, and fill with knobs of butter, a little cream cheese or soured cream.

*Potato and leek soup

Serves 6
This soup is the basis for Vichyssoise —a delicious cold vegetable soup (see below).

2 onions
2 oz butter
2 tbsp oil
1 clove crushed garlic
1 large leek
1 lb potatoes
1½ pints chicken stock
seasoning
2 tbsp chopped parsley

Peel and slice the onion. Fry in the melted butter and oil with the

crushed garlic for 5 minutes. Add the washed and sliced leek and the peeled and sliced potatoes and cook gently for a further 5 minutes. Add the stock, seasoning and chopped parsley. Bring to the boil. Cover the pan and simmer gently for 35–40 minutes. The ingredients thicken the soup during cooking without the addition of flour. If you prefer a smoother soup, blend or sieve the ingredients, and stir in a little cream.

For Vichyssoise: omit the chopped parsley. Chill the sieved soup, with a generous amount of cream stirred in. Top with chopped chives before serving. This soup is excellent for freezing.

(American: ¼ cup butter, 3 cups sliced potato, 3 cups chicken stock)

Special potato crisps

Serves 4–6
3 medium size potatoes
oil for deep frying
celery salt
paprika

Peel the potatoes and cut into wafer thin slices, using a mandolin or potato peeler. Pat dry on a clean tea towel. Put into the basket of a deep fryer, and lower into the hot deep fat. Fry until crisp and golden. Do not fry too many crisps at once: it's better to do them in two or three separate lots. Drain very thoroughly on absorbent paper, and sprinkle with celery salt and paprika while they are still warm.

*Potato and avocado cream

Serves 4
$\frac{1}{2}$ lb potatoes
1 oz butter
1 avocado pear
seasoning
1 clove crushed garlic
4 tbsp thick cream

Peel the potatoes, and cut into pieces. Cook in salted water until just tender. Drain the potatoes. Mash with the butter while still warm. Peel, halve and stone the avocado. Mash the avocado flesh until smooth. Mix the avocado puree with the mashed potato, seasoning, crushed garlic and cream. Chill. Serve as a starter with fingers of hot toast.

(American: 1 cup mashed potato, 2 tbsp butter)

Minted potato salad

Serves 4
1 lb potatoes
chicken stock
5 tbsp oil
2 tbsp vinegar
1 tbsp mint jelly
seasoning

Peel the potatoes and cut into $\frac{1}{4}$ in thick slices. Put into a pan, and add sufficient stock to just cover. Bring to the boil. Cover the pan and simmer until just tender. Drain. Mix the oil with the vinegar, mint jelly and seasoning, and spoon over the warm potatoes. Leave until cool, and then chill. This potato dish is particularly good with hot or cold lamb. If you have no mint jelly, a little mint sauce or chopped mint can be used instead.

(American: 3 cups sliced potato)

Dauphine potatoes

Serves 4–6
$\frac{3}{4}$ lb potatoes
seasoning
1 oz grated Parmesan cheese
2 oz butter
$\frac{1}{4}$ pint water
$2\frac{1}{2}$ oz plain flour
2 eggs
oil for deep frying

Peel the potatoes and cut into pieces. Cook in salted water until just tender. Drain the potatoes, and mash, with a little butter and cream, if liked, but do not make the mixture too soft. Add the seasoning and Parmesan cheese. Put the butter and water into a pan. Heat until just melted. Add the flour and beat until the mixture leaves the sides of the pan—there should be enough heat retained in the pan to do this off the cooker. Allow to cool slightly, and gradually add the beaten eggs. Combine with the mashed potato. Carefully drop spoonfuls of the mixture into a pan of hot deep fat. Fry until puffed and golden. The potatoes will need turning in the fat halfway through cooking. Drain and serve immediately.

(American: $1\frac{1}{2}$ cups mashed potato, 1 tbsp grated Parmesan cheese, $\frac{1}{4}$ cup butter, $\frac{1}{2}$ cup water, 5 tbsp plain flour)

*Danish potato duchesse

Serves 6
$\frac{3}{4}$ lb potatoes
$\frac{1}{3}$ pint thick apple puree
2 egg yolks
2 tbsp soured cream
pinch grated nutmeg
seasoning

Peel the potatoes and cut into pieces. Cook in salted water until just tender. Drain the potatoes and mash, with a little butter and cream if liked. Mix the mashed potato with the apple puree, egg yolks, cream, nutmeg and seasoning. Using a star piping nozzle, pipe the mixture into small pyramids on greased baking sheets. Bake at 375°F, Mark 5, for 30–35 minutes. These special duchesse potatoes are delicious with hot pork dishes.

(American: $1\frac{1}{2}$ cups mashed potato, $\frac{2}{3}$ cup apple puree)

*Normandy potatoes

Serves 4
1 lb potatoes
chicken stock
seasoning
1 apple
$\frac{1}{4}$ pint double cream
1 oz butter

Peel the potatoes and cut into $\frac{1}{8}$ in thick slices. Put the potatoes into a pan and add sufficient stock to just cover. Season. Bring to the boil, cover the pan, and simmer for 10 minutes. Drain the potatoes. Arrange them overlapping, in a greased ovenproof dish. Core and grate the apple. Mix the apple with the cream, and spoon over the sliced potatoes. Dot the surface with butter. Bake at 375°F, Mark 5, for 25 minutes.

(American: 3 cups sliced potatoes, $\frac{1}{2}$ cup double cream, 2 tbsp butter)

Devilled potatoes

Serves 4
1 lb tiny new potatoes
$1\frac{1}{2}$ oz butter
2 teasp dry mustard
1 tbsp tomato puree
2 tbsp chutney
2 tbsp vinegar
3 teasp Worcestershire sauce
seasoning

Scrape the new potatoes. Parboil in

salted water for 10 minutes. Drain thoroughly. Melt the butter. Stir in the mustard, tomato puree, chutney, vinegar, Worcestershire sauce and seasoning. Simmer for 5 minutes. Add the potatoes. Cover the pan and cook gently for 12–15 minutes; if the heat is too high, the potatoes will stick.

(American: 3 cups new potatoes, 3 tbsp butter, any brown sauce instead of Worcestershire)

*Curried potatoes

Serves 4
1 lb potatoes
1 onion
1 clove crushed garlic
3 tbsp oil
1 tbsp curry powder
1 tbsp flour
$\frac{1}{2}$ pint beef stock
1 tbsp tomato puree
2 oz sultanas
seasoning

Peel the potatoes and cut into cubes. Put into a bowl of cold water to prevent discoloration. Peel and slice the onion. Fry in the oil with the garlic for 5 minutes. Add the curry powder and cook for 1 minute. Stir in the flour and cook for a further minute. Gradually stir in the beef stock, tomato puree, sultanas and seasoning. Bring to the boil and simmer for 10 minutes. Add the

drained cubed potato and simmer for a further 20–25 minutes. Serve either as a vegetable or as a dish on its own with rice.

(American: 3 cups cubed potato, 1 cup beef stock, $\frac{1}{4}$ cup sultanas)

*Potato cheese balls

Serves 4
$\frac{3}{4}$ lb potatoes
2 egg yolks
3 oz Gouda cheese
flour
beaten egg
breadcrumbs

Peel the potatoes and cut into pieces. Boil in salted water until just tender. Drain thoroughly. Mash the potato, and beat in the egg yolks. Chill the mixture, to firm up slightly. Form the potato into small balls, about the size of a large plum. Cut the cheese into small cubes. Press a cube of cheese into each and mould the potato round to enclose the cheese completely. Chill for 1 hour. Dip into flour and beaten egg, and coat with crumbs. Lower the potato and cheese balls into a pan of deep fat and fry until crisp and golden. Drain well. Season to taste.
Freeze before deep frying.

(American: $1\frac{1}{2}$ cups mashed potato, $\frac{2}{3}$ cup cubed Gouda cheese)

Jamaican sugared potatoes

Serves 4
1 lb tiny new potatoes
2 oz butter
4 tbsp clear honey
1 oz soft brown sugar
seasoning

Scrape the new potatoes. Put into a pan with salted water. Parboil for 10 minutes. Drain thoroughly. Heat the melted butter with the honey. Add the scraped new potatoes. Cover the pan and cook gently for 15–20 minutes, shaking from time to time to coat the potatoes. Add the brown sugar and simmer for a further 5 minutes.

(American: 3 cups new potatoes, $\frac{1}{4}$ cup butter, 1 tbsp soft brown sugar)

Souffle jacket potatoes

Serves 4
4 large potatoes
$1\frac{1}{2}$ oz butter
2 eggs
2 oz grated cheese
seasoning

Bake the potatoes in their jackets until tender (see p 47). Cut a slice from the top of each potato. Scoop out most of the centre cooked potato carefully. Mix the potato pulp with butter, egg yolks, grated cheese and seasoning. Whisk the egg whites stiffly, and fold into the potato mixture. Spoon back into the potato skins. Bake at 400°F, Mark 6, for 20–25 minutes, until the potato filling is puffed and golden.

(American: 3 tbsp butter, 2 tbsp grated cheese)

*Potato and chestnut croquettes

Serves 4
$\frac{3}{4}$ lb potatoes
6 oz chestnut puree
seasoning
1 tbsp redcurrant jelly
flour
beaten egg
chopped nuts

Peel the potatoes and cut into pieces. Boil in salted water until just tender. Drain thoroughly. Mash the potato. Mix the mashed potato with the chestnut puree, seasoning and redcurrant jelly. Form into cylindrical croquette shapes. Chill for 1 hour. Dip into flour and beaten egg, and coat evenly with chopped nuts. Lower the croquettes into a pan of hot fat and deep fry until crisp and golden. Drain well. *Freeze before deep frying.*

(American: $1\frac{1}{2}$ cups mashed potato, $\frac{2}{3}$ cup chestnut puree)

*Potato and spinach cakes

Serves 6
1 lb potatoes
6 oz cooked drained spinach or
    frozen spinach puree, well drained
seasoning
grated rind ½ lemon
2 egg yolks
oil or melted butter

Peel the potatoes and cut into pieces.
Boil in salted water until just tender.
Drain. Mash potatoes. Mix the
mashed potato with the cooked
spinach, seasoning, grated lemon
rind and egg yolks. Form into small
round cakes. Chill for 1 hour. Heat
enough oil or melted butter in a
frying pan to just cover the bottom.
Add the cakes, three at a time, and
fry until cooked and brown on the
underside. Flip the cakes over, and
cook on the other side.
Freeze cakes uncooked.

(American: 2 cups mashed potato,
1 cup cooked spinach)

Potato and sweetcorn skillet cake

Serves 4
*This is an ideal dish for campers or
those with a barbecue; it can be
cooked over an open flame, out of
doors.*

3 large potatoes
medium size can sweetcorn
seasoning
2 eggs
2 tbsp cream
1 oz butter
1 tbsp oil

Peel the potatoes. Grate the potatoes
coarsely. Mix the grated potato with
the sweetcorn, seasoning, beaten
eggs and cream. Heat the butter and
oil in a frying pan. Pour in the potato
and sweetcorn mixture. Cook
without stirring until the mixture is
set on the underside (stirring the
mixture will scramble it). Using a
slice, carefully turn the 'cake' over.
Cook until the other side is set and
brown. Cut the skillet cake into
4 wedges, and serve immediately.

This cake is delicious with cold
meats, or turned into a one-pan
supper dish with the addition of
chopped bacon or grated cheese.

(American: 2 tbsp butter, 1 cup
sweetcorn kernels)

*Potato scones

Makes approx 12
¾ lb potatoes
1 teasp dry mustard
6 oz flour
2 oz butter
seasoning
2 tbsp chopped parsley

Peel the potatoes and cut into pieces.
Boil in salted water until just tender.

Drain well. Mash the potato. Mix the mashed potato with the dry mustard, sieved flour, melted butter, seasoning and chopped parsley. Chill the mixture for 1 hour. Roll out gently on a floured surface, and cut into 12 triangles. The scones can either be cooked on a greased griddle or in a lightly greased solid frying pan. Cook on one side until lightly golden, then flip the scones over, and cook on the other side. Serve hot with butter.

(American: $1\frac{1}{2}$ cups mashed potato, $1\frac{1}{2}$ cups flour, $\frac{1}{4}$ cup butter)

Herbed potato loaf

Serves 6
$1\frac{1}{2}$ lb potatoes
3 egg yolks
1 oz butter
3 oz breadcrumbs
2 teasp mixed dried herbs
seasoning

Peel the potatoes, and cut into pieces. Boil in salted water until just tender. Drain well. Mash the potato. Mix the mashed potato with the egg yolks, melted butter, breadcrumbs, herbs and seasoning. Spoon the mixture into a greased and lined loaf tin. Press the mixture down evenly. Bake at 375°F, Mark 5, for about 40 minutes. Leave to cool slightly in the tin. Unmould the loaf, and serve cut into slices.

(American: 3 cups mashed potato, 2 tbsp butter, $\frac{1}{2}$ cup breadcrumbs)

Potato and onion gratin

Serves 4
2 onions
4 tbsp oil
3 large potatoes
seasoning
3 rashers streaky bacon
5 tbsp cream
2 oz grated cheese

Peel and slice the onion. Fry in the oil for 5 minutes. Peel and slice the potatoes quite thinly. Add the sliced potato to the onion, and fry together until the potatoes are lightly golden on both sides. Season to taste, and spoon into a greased ovenproof dish. Scatter the chopped bacon over the surface. Spoon over the cream, and sprinkle with grated cheese. Bake at 375°F, Mark 5, for 35–40 minutes.

(American: 2 tbsp grated cheese)

Tomatoes

Tomatoes, the ever-popular rosy red fruit, were discovered in South America by the Spaniards, and brought to Europe more than 400 years ago. They have been essential to Mediterranean cookery ever since, for making the rich fruity sauces which are the bases of so many Mediterranean dishes.

The first tomatoes were little bigger than currants, and in no way resembled the juicy-fleshed fruit that we know today. They used to be called love apples by the French, and golden apples by the Italians, and many people considered them to have aphrodisiac properties!

Before the nineteenth century, the more northern countries of Europe, including England, regarded tomatoes with suspicion, condemning them as the cause of many serious illnesses. They gained popularity in Britain from the middle of the nineteenth century, when they began to be grown in this country.

The most popular varieties of tomato are

the 'common' tomato: round and regular in shape and colour; mainly grown in England, the Channel Islands, Holland, and the Canaries;

the 'plum' tomato: pear-shaped, and only growing in hot climates; these tomatoes are usually bought canned in this country, and the fresh variety are only sold by continental greengrocers;

the 'cherry' tomato: miniature tomatoes which grow in clusters; they are ideal for salads and starters, as they can be used whole;

Italian and Spanish tomatoes: craggy, misshapen tomatoes with a rich sweet flavour; they are among the best for their taste, but many housewives avoid them because of their strange shape.

Tomatoes are generally available all the year round. Most British-grown tomatoes are produced in hothouses, and they have a long season. It normally begins in March, and lasts through until November. Imported tomatoes supplement our own supplies. Italian and Spanish tomatoes are usually sold by continental greengrocers in this country and can also sometimes be bought in markets, where they are cheaper.

Tomatoes perish quite quickly, especially if they are bruised. It is advisable to buy firm, even under-ripe tomatoes, and to use them within three to four days. Keep them either in a well ventilated vegetable rack in a cool place, or in the 'crisper' drawer of the refrigerator. Make sure that you do not stand heavier vegetables on top of them, as they squash very easily. Remove any damaged ones and use them immediately.

Tomatoes have the most stable nutritional value of all vegetables, mainly because they are eaten raw, more frequently than they are cooked, and so their rich supply of vitamin C is retained.

Tomatoes have a subtle flavour, and seasoning and added flavourings are very important—strong foods can spoil their taste. Most tomato recipes are enhanced by a pinch of sugar, and the addition of a few chopped herbs: oregano and basil are the best.

For salads, choose firm tomatoes. Slice and marinate them in a delicately flavoured dressing of orange or lemon juice, oil and a little chopped mint. Season lightly. Fruit juice makes a better dressing than vinegar, unless you happen to like the strong piquancy of vinegar.

When cooking tomatoes, choose really firm ones for baking whole or for stuffing and use the cheaper, over-ripe tomatoes for soups, sauces and casseroles.

*Chilled tomato soup

Serves 6
This recipe makes a tomato soup that tastes as it should, full of the fresh fruity tomato flavour.

1 onion
1 clove crushed garlic
1 oz butter
2 tbsp oil
$1\frac{1}{2}$ lb tomatoes, blanched and
    skinned (see tomato jam, p 62)
a little chopped fresh or dried basil
$1\frac{1}{4}$ pints chicken stock
1 teasp sugar
seasoning
pinch grated nutmeg
$\frac{1}{4}$ pint soured cream
chopped parsley

Peel and slice the onion. Fry the onion and crushed garlic in butter and oil for 3 minutes. Add the roughly chopped tomatoes and fry gently for a further 3 minutes. Add the basil, chicken stock, sugar, seasoning and grated nutmeg. Bring the soup to the boil. Cover the pan and simmer gently for 30 minutes. Push the soup through a sieve, or blend in a liquidizer. Stir the soured cream into the warm soup. Chill for 3–4 hours. Serve in small glass bowls with an ice cube in each, and sprinkle with chopped parsley.

For decorative ice cubes to float in the soup: put a Spanish olive into each section of the ice tray, and fill up with cold water. Freeze until solid. Unmould in the usual way.

(American: 2 tbsp butter, 3 cups chopped tomato, $2\frac{1}{2}$ cups chicken stock, $\frac{1}{2}$ cup soured cream)

*Tomatoes en gelee

Serves 4
6 tomatoes, skinned (see tomato
    jam, p 62)
seasoning
2 tbsp chopped parsley
1 can consomme
1 tbsp sherry
4 tbsp soured cream
little chopped onion

Halve the tomatoes and remove the seeds. Chop quite finely. Divide the tomato amongst 4 individual dishes. Season to taste, and sprinkle with chopped parsley. Mix the consomme with the sherry and spoon over the chopped tomato. Chill until set. Top each dish with a little soured cream and sprinkle with chopped onion. Serve with fingers of hot toast.

Instead of consomme you can use $\frac{3}{4}$ pint chicken stock, mixed with $\frac{1}{3}$ oz dissolved gelatine.

(American: $1\frac{1}{2}$ cups consomme)

Seafood tomatoes

Serves 4
4 large tomatoes
small jar mussels
2 oz peeled prawns
1 ripe avocado
$\frac{1}{4}$ pint mayonnaise (see p 15)
4 tbsp cream
1 tbsp tomato puree
grated rind $\frac{1}{2}$ lemon
seasoning
small lettuce leaves
cayenne pepper
parsley

Choose tomatoes that are even in shape and nice and firm. Cut a thin slice from the top of each tomato and carefully scoop out the centre. (There is no need to waste the centre from the tomatoes; save it to use in soups and sauces.) Turn the hollowed tomatoes upside down on a piece of absorbent paper to drain. Mix the drained mussels with half the peeled prawns and the peeled and chopped avocado. Mix the mayonnaise with the cream, tomato puree, lemon rind and seasoning. Bind the fish and avocado with 4 tbsp of the sauce. Spoon into the hollowed tomatoes. Arrange the stuffed tomatoes on a bed of shredded lettuce. Spoon over the remaining sauce, and decorate with the reserved prawns. Sprinkle with a little cayenne pepper and garnish with a few sprigs of parsley.

(American: $\frac{1}{2}$ cup mussels, $\frac{1}{3}$ cup peeled prawns, $\frac{1}{2}$ cup mayonnaise)

Piquant tomatoes

Serves 4
1 onion
1 large carrot
$\frac{1}{3}$ pint chicken stock
3 teasp made mustard
3 teasp Worcestershire sauce
juice 1 lemon
1 tbsp brown sugar
seasoning
3 tbsp fruit chutney
1 tbsp tomato puree
6 medium sized tomatoes
oil or melted butter

Peel the onion and the carrot, and grate coarsely. Put the carrot and onion into a pan with the stock. Simmer gently for 10 minutes. Add the mustard, Worcestershire sauce, lemon juice, brown sugar, seasoning, fruit chutney, and tomato puree. Simmer gently for a further 15 minutes. This should give a coating-consistency sauce.
Cut the tomatoes in half, and brush the cut surfaces with melted butter or oil. Grill the tomatoes until just tender; do not have the grill too hot or the tomatoes will disintegrate. Spoon the hot sauce over the tomatoes and serve immediately.

(American: $\frac{2}{3}$ cup chicken stock, any brown sauce)

*Tomates aux amandes

Serves 4
6 firm tomatoes
juice 1 orange
seasoning
1 clove crushed garlic
6 tbsp oil
6 tbsp cream
2 oz ground almonds
1½ oz flaked almonds
1 oz butter

Slice the tomatoes and put into a greased shallow ovenproof dish. Mix the orange juice with the seasoning, crushed garlic and oil. Spoon over the sliced tomato. Leave in the refrigerator to marinate, covered, for 3–4 hours. Drain off the marinade, and mix with the cream and the ground almonds. Spoon over the tomato. Sprinkle with the flaked almonds and dot the surface with butter. Bake at 375°F, Mark 5, for 25–30 minutes.
This recipe has an interesting sweet nutty flavour and is particularly good served with fried or grilled fish.

(American: 3 tbsp ground almonds, 2 tbsp flaked almonds, 2 tbsp butter)

Pain grille aux tomates

Serves 6
2 cloves crushed garlic
1 can anchovy fillets
1 tbsp olive oil
juice ½ lemon
seasoning
6 thick slices bread
6 large tomatoes
oil or melted butter
3 oz Philadelphia cream cheese, or
    similar

Pound the crushed garlic with the drained chopped anchovy fillets and stir in the olive oil to give a smooth paste. Add the lemon juice and the seasoning to taste. Remove the crusts from the bread. Toast the bread on one side only. Spread the anchovy and garlic paste on the untoasted side while the bread is still warm, so that it absorbs the highly flavoured paste. Slice the tomatoes and arrange on top of the toast. Brush with a little oil or melted butter. If you like a strong anchovy flavour, use the oil drained from the canned anchovies. Bake at 375°F, Mark 5, for about 20 minutes. Serve very hot, topped with knobs of cream cheese.

(American: ⅓ cup cream cheese)

Tomato scramble

Serves 4
6 eggs
2 teasp Worcestershire sauce
seasoning
little garlic salt
1½ oz butter
4 large tomatoes, blanched and

skinned (see tomato jam, p 62)
3 tbsp double cream
4 slices buttered toast

Beat the eggs with the Worcestershire sauce, seasoning and garlic salt. Melt the butter in a pan. Add the egg mixture, and stir over a gentle heat until the mixture forms soft creamy flakes. Stir in the seeded and chopped tomatoes and the cream, and stir over the heat for 30 seconds. Spoon on to the hot toast and serve immediately.

(American: 3 tbsp butter, any brown sauce in place of Worcestershire sauce)

Tomato soufflé

Serves 4
1 oz butter
$1\frac{1}{2}$ oz plain flour
$\frac{1}{2}$ teasp dry mustard
$\frac{1}{3}$ pint milk
$1\frac{1}{2}$ tbsp tomato puree
seasoning
4 eggs
$1\frac{1}{2}$ oz grated Parmesan cheese
6 tomatoes, blanched and skinned
   (see Tomato jam, p 62)

Grease a $1\frac{1}{2}$ pint soufflé dish thoroughly. This is very important if the soufflé is to rise properly and not stick to the dish. Melt the butter in a pan. Stir in the flour and mustard and cook for 1 minute. Gradually stir in the milk. Bring to the boil to thicken, beating to give a smooth sauce. Simmer for 3 minutes. Remove from the heat and beat in the tomato puree, seasoning, egg yolks and $\frac{2}{3}$ of the Parmesan cheese. Beat the egg whites until they stand in stiff peaks. Fold little by little, very gently with a metal spoon, into the sauce. Fold in the chopped seeded tomatoes. Turn into the prepared soufflé dish. Sprinkle the top with the remaining cheese. Bake on the middle shelf of the oven at 400°F, Mark 6, for 25–30 minutes. Serve immediately.

If you prefer a soufflé that is a little more moist, and not quite so crusty, stand the soufflé dish in a roasting tin containing sufficient water to come halfway up the side of the dish. This prevents the soufflé drying as it cooks by regulating the heat.

Tomato and pepper sauce (see p 62) is particularly good served with this soufflé.

(American: 2 tbsp butter, 3 tbsp plain flour, $\frac{2}{3}$ cup milk, 2 tbsp grated Parmesan cheese)

*Cheesy topped tomatoes

Serves 4
6 tomatoes
1 onion
1 oz butter

1 oz flour
½ pint milk
seasoning
3 oz grated cheese
2 tbsp crisp breadcrumbs
1 oz butter

Slice the tomatoes. Peel and coarsely grate the onion. Arrange the tomato and onions in layers in a greased ovenproof dish. Melt the butter in a pan. Add the flour and cook for 1 minute. Gradually stir in the milk. Bring to the boil to thicken, beating to give a smooth sauce. Simmer for 3 minutes. Season to taste and add ⅔ of the cheese. Spoon over the tomato and onion. Sprinkle with the crisp breadcrumbs and the remaining grated cheese. Dot the surface with butter. Bake at 375°F, Mark 5, for 30–35 minutes.

(American: 2 tbsp butter, 2 tbsp flour, generous cup of milk, ½ cup grated cheese, 2 tbsp butter)

Tomato clafouti

Serves 4
Clafouti *is the French name given to a baked batter, either sweet or savoury.*

8 tomatoes
3 tbsp oil
4 oz plain flour
seasoning
1 egg
½ pint milk
1½ oz grated Parmesan cheese

Halve the tomatoes and put into a shallow ovenproof dish. Spoon over the oil. Put into the oven, 425°F, Mark 7, for 3–4 minutes. Beat the sieved flour and seasoning with the egg and milk to give a smooth batter. Stir in the grated cheese and pour over the tomatoes. Return to the oven until well risen and golden: about 25–30 minutes.

(American: generous cup of flour, 1 cup milk, 2 tbsp grated Parmesan cheese)

*Tomato fondue

Serves 6
1 large onion
1 clove crushed garlic
2 oz butter
2 tbsp oil
1 lb tomatoes
little chopped fresh or dried basil
1 tbsp tomato puree
1 teasp sugar
1 pint red wine
seasoning
¼ pint double cream
cubes of ham, cheese, salami, or
    other cooked meat

Peel and chop the onion. Fry the chopped onion and crushed garlic in the butter and oil for 5 minutes. Add the chopped tomatoes and herbs and cook for a further 5 minutes. Stir in the tomato puree, sugar, red wine and seasoning. Bring to the boil and simmer for 20 minutes. Stir in the cream and reheat; do not allow the fondue to boil. Serve hot with the cubed meats and cheese for dipping. If you have a table warmer or fondue burner, stand a casserole of the tomato fondue on top.

(American: 1½ cups chopped tomato, ¼ cup butter, 2 cups red wine, ½ cup cream)

Casseroled tomatoes

Serves 6
1 onion
2 tbsp oil
1½ oz butter
3 rashers lean bacon
1 tbsp flour
½ pint red wine
¼ pint beef stock
1 teasp sugar
seasoning
1½ lb tomatoes, blanched and skinned (see tomato jam, p 62)

Peel and chop the onion. Fry in the oil and butter for 3 minutes. Add the chopped bacon and fry for a further 3 minutes. Stir in the flour, and cook for 1 minute. Gradually add the red wine and the stock. Bring to the boil and simmer for 2 minutes. Add the sugar and seasoning to taste. Put the skinned tomatoes into a shallow casserole. Pour the wine sauce over the top. Cover the casserole with a

lid. Cook at 350°F, Mark 4, for 35–40 minutes.

If you prefer a thicker sauce, use 2 tbsp flour for thickening.

Serve as a supper dish with fresh crusty bread, or as an accompanying vegetable.

(American: 3 cups tomatoes, 3 tbsp butter, generous cup red wine, ½ cup stock)

Country baked tomatoes

Serves 4
4 large tomatoes prepared as in Seafood tomatoes (see p 57)
4 oz sausagemeat
1 small onion
2 tbsp breadcrumbs
seasoning
1 teasp mixed herbs
1 teasp made mustard
1 egg yolk
¼ pint soured cream
2 oz grated cheese
chopped parsley
toast triangles

Prepare the tomatoes. Mix the sausagemeat with the peeled and grated onion, breadcrumbs, seasoning, herbs, mustard and egg yolk. Press the savoury filling into the hollowed tomatoes. Put into a greased shallow ovenproof dish. Spoon the soured cream over the top, and sprinkle with the grated cheese. Bake at 350°F, Mark 4, for 40–45 minutes. Sprinkle with a little chopped parsley and garnish with triangles of toast.

(American: $\frac{1}{2}$ cup sausagemeat, $\frac{1}{2}$ cup soured cream, $\frac{1}{3}$ cup grated cheese)

*Tomato jam

Makes approximately 4 lb
This is an ideal recipe for using up over-ripe tomatoes. They can also be bought cheaply especially for the recipe.

3 lb over-ripe tomatoes
juice and grated rind 2 lemons
3$\frac{1}{2}$ lb granulated sugar

Nick the skin of each tomato. Put the tomatoes into a bowl, and cover with boiling water. Leave to stand for 2–3 minutes. Remove them from the water and peel back the skins. Quarter the peeled tomatoes and put into a large pan with the lemon juice and the grated rind. Bring to a gentle boil and simmer until pulpy. Add the sugar and stir to dissolve. Bring back to the boil and cook over a moderate heat, until the jam reaches setting point: put a little of the jam on to a cold saucer, and drag a finger across the surface. It should form a wrinkled skin. Put the jam into warm clean jars and cover. If you want a redder jam, add a little red food colouring with the sugar.

Variations: add a little chopped stem ginger; substitute 1 lb tart apples for 1 lb of tomatoes; or make the jam more like a chutney by adding a couple of coarsely grated onions.

For tomato curd: cook the tomatoes as above until pulpy. Put them into a bowl over a pan of hot water, with 2 lb sugar, 6oz butter and 4 egg yolks. Stir over a gentle heat until the curd will coat the back of a wooden spoon—it should be quite thick. Put into jars and seal. This tomato curd has a shorter shelf life than the jam because of the egg and butter content. Do not keep it for more than 8 weeks, and store it in a cool dry place.

(American: 6 cups quartered tomatoes, 8 cups granulated sugar for the tomato jam; 6 cups quartered tomatoes, 4 cups sugar, $\frac{3}{4}$ cup butter for the tomato curd)

*Tomato and pepper sauce

Serves 6
This is rather similar in flavour to ratatouille, but much thinner in consistency. It is another recipe using over-ripe tomatoes.

2 onions
1 clove crushed garlic
2 tbsp oil
1 oz butter
1 lb tomatoes
1 green pepper

$\frac{1}{4}$ pint water or white wine
3 tbsp vinegar
2 oz raisins
seasoning

Peel and chop the onion. Fry the chopped onion and the crushed garlic in the oil and butter for 5 minutes. Add the chopped tomatoes, the chopped and seeded pepper, vinegar, raisins and seasoning. Stir in the water; or use white wine for an even better flavour (keep left-over white and red wines in corked bottles, for using in sauces, casseroles, etc.). Simmer the sauce gently for 20–25 minutes. If the sauce becomes too thick, add a little extra water or wine.

This sauce is delicious with grilled chops and chicken joints or with fish. The sauce will keep in the refrigerator for up to 10 days.

(American: 2 tbsp butter, 2 cups chopped tomato, $\frac{1}{4}$ cup raisins, $\frac{1}{4}$ cup water or wine)

Index